ANTI-SEMITISM

ALSO BY THEODORE ISAAC RUBIN:
Lisa and David
Compassion and Self-Hate
Real Love

ANTI-SEMITISM

A DISEASE OF THE MIND

Theodore Isaac Rubin, M.D.
author of *The Angry Book* and *Compassion and Hate*

Skyhorse Publishing

Skyhorse Publishing books may be purchased in bulk at special discounts for sales promotion, corporate gifts, fund-raising, or educational purposes. Special editions can also be created to specifications. For details, contact the Special Sales Department, Skyhorse Publishing, 307 West 36th Street, 11th Floor, New York, NY 10018 or info@skyhorsepublishing.com.

Skyhorse® and Skyhorse Publishing® are registered trademarks of Skyhorse Publishing, Inc.®, a Delaware corporation.

Visit our website at www.skyhorsepublishing.com.

10 9 8 7 6 5 4 3 2 1

Library of Congress Cataloging-in-Publication Data is available on file.

Cover design by Rain Saukas

Print ISBN: 978-1-62914-453-5
Ebook ISBN: 978-1-62914-858-8

Printed in the United States of America

CONTENTS

ACKNOWLEDGMENTS

In loving memory of my father, Nathan, whose own father was murdered in a pogrom in the Ukraine.

I would like to thank Dr. Louis de Rosis for his encouragement. His own interest in the subject will surely cast much light.

Many thanks to Dr. Marvin Weitz for support and constant reminders of the importance of this investigation.

I would like to thank Dr. Robert Schuller, a great Christian, for his kind words and concern with this most difficult problem.

AUTHOR'S NOTE

It is of utmost importance to note that this book is in no way a criticism of Christianity.

Indeed, it is not possible for a Christian to be an anti-Semite or an anti-Semite to be a Christian. Bigotry, including anti-Semitism, and Christianity are antithetical. The disease called anti-Semitism destroys Christian principles and values as it promotes chronic hatred and inhumanity.

Unfortunately, stereotyping, bigotry, prejudice, discrimination, and ethnic murder continue virtually unabated.

The projection of self-hate is easy, especially so by highly suggestible people. Ruthless, manipulative psychopaths know that hate, in its sick way, binds people in efforts to destroy perceived enemies. Using this psychological dynamic is commonplace for power-hungry fearmongers. Killing the "parent religion" is insanely and unconsciously believed to be a self-freeing "process."

Hating Jews is very much in evidence now as ever, and is a major player in this contagious, malignant disease.

However, there is little research dedicated to insight or remediation as regards this dangerous malady. Even following the Holocaust, the disease is ever present.

This book is about Jew hatred, but much of it applies to irrational hatred of any group. Perhaps shedding some light on the possible dynamics of this illness will awaken interest in the problem as well as motivation to understand and eradicate it.

Theodore Isaac Rubin
New York City, 2008

PREFACE

My interest in anti-Semitism is rooted in my identification. Let me identify myself!

I am a human being. I am a father and grandfather. I am a Jew, and I am a psychiatrist.

As a human being I am deeply concerned with the eradication of bigotry wherever it exists.

As a Jew I have experienced personal hurt, pain, and fear as a consequence of Jew hating. Many of my most painful memories go back to early childhood—yes, here in America where I was born!

As a father and grandfather I am concerned for all children regardless of religion or color. I would like them to be free of the disease of bigotry. I am convinced that bigotry constricts and destroys the hosts as well as their victims.

As a psychiatrist I am concerned that we are in fact dealing with a disease—a malignant emotional illness. Eradication of this, as with other illness, cannot be accomplished without understanding. Since this is a psychiatric illness it is necessary to understand the psychodynamics involved. I have developed the system I call *symbol sickness* in order to facilitate understanding these dynamics. Symbol sickness is especially applicable to all bigotry illness. But it can also help to understand any emotional illness. For example, I deal here rather extensively with envy, one of the most self-corrosive of human emotional poisons. This system and the dynamics of anti-Semitism are the result of much clinical experience, personal experience, and thought. This problem has been on my mind nearly all my life. As a child I could not understand why people hated me and my family only because we were Jews. Later on I found out other groups were hated, too.

But I also found out that anti-Semitism has a history almost as old as Western Civilization itself. As with other diseases, it has gone through periods of relative quiescence as well as acute and severe flare-ups. It has been decidedly chronic (never having gone away), pandemic (worldwide), and incredibly destructive. Socioeconomic, political, and historical dynamics play a role and have been written about extensively. But there has been very little done in terms of psychodynamics. I hope to fill this gap a bit and to encourage others in this endeavor because I fervently believe we are in fact dealing with a disease of the mind. Unfortunately people sick with this disease can be very dangerous and even murderous but are not treated accordingly. Understanding this disease and these people will, I hope, make some contribution to preventing another Holocaust—the ultimate horror. I also hope it will help to stop the victimization of all people who are the victims of bigotry all their lives.

I shall summarize my goals in the next few pages.

GOALS

We are all familiar with the disturbance. It seems to have always been with us. It is pandemic, having touched multitudes of people in every corner of the globe.

Its effects are devastating. It ravages its hosts and its hosts destroy their victims.

It is metastatic, attacking every area of our lives. Even as it springs from emotional disturbance, it feeds emotional disturbance.

I believe that Jew hating or anti-Semitism is a nonorganic disease of the mind. I believe that it cannot be understood or eradicated unless it is viewed as the grievous psychodynamic disorder that it is.

Though there are, as in all emotional illnesses, sociopolitical, economic factors, and effects, this is primarily a psychiatric problem. Unfortunately, it is not contained as such in the various compendiums of psychiatric syndromes. It does not appear in the *Statistical Manual of Mental Disorders,* Third Edition or later editions.

As with all other psychiatric disturbances, here, too neurotic, psychotic, and sociopathic mechanisms abound. Projection, paranoia, phobias, rationalization, thought disorder, delusions, compartmentalization, and all other "defenses" are commonplace. But, as with other psychiatric illnesses, these neurotic and psychotic defenses come together in a particular combination so as to make the illness unmistakenly identifiable.

This illness, however, of all its siblings, reaches the most people, is the most contagious, the most destructive, and the most difficult to treat and eradicate. But it is not hopeless! However, treatment cannot be effective unless we recognize that we are in fact dealing with psychiatric pathology and that we must continue the struggle to understand the psychodynamics involved. Medication will help! The organically sound mind is capable of producing behavior infinitely more bizarre and destructive than the organically brain-damaged mind.

Elucidation of the sickness, as in the case of all emotional illness, must shed light on other psychiatric disturbances (especially bigotry) since they are all interconnected and overlap. A study of this illness is unique, however, in the opportunity it affords to view the interconnections of culture and personal psychodynamics. I believe this combination of personal history and cultural forces is present in all disturbances as it is in normal behavior.

I do not want to recapitulate a study of psychiatric mechanisms in this work. But it is necessary to understand some of them here and my own ideas about them in order to view the germinating ground of the illness. I shall devote the first part of this book to these underpinnings, but my major interest is, of course, the unique aspects of the illness itself.

I believe that we are all familiar enough with Jew hating that a detailed description is not necessary.

Suffice it to say here that:

- The illness could not exist without the complete panoply of roots of all emotional disturbance.

- The illness exists in various forms of intensity from subtle neurotic manifestations to blatantly and murderously psychotic acting out.

- More than other illnesses it devastates people who are victims of its infected victims. It always cripples their self-esteem, if nothing else, and, as we all know, also is capable of engendering great suffering, horror, and murder.

Its socioeconomic, political effects are more far-reaching and devastating than all other emotional diseases combined.

This book is not a research project. It is largely perceptive, reflective, and speculative. I hope it encourages further speculation, investigation, and even proofs.

Of course, this book will I hope inevitably tell something of the truth about Jews and who they are and what they feel.

PART I

1 > THE GERMINATING GROUND

As I have already indicated, the stuff of all extant kinds of neurosis—anxiety, repressed anger, low self-esteem, insecurity, etc.—as well as neurotic defenses—displacement, projection, rationalization, alienation, compartmentalization, etc.—all provide fertile grounds for this illness as they do for others.

But in this section I want to describe several emotional dynamics that especially provide a rich germinating flora for the sickness to root and to flourish.

These dynamics eventually combine with special, directly linked emotional vectors as I shall describe late on. The two groups work as a symbiotic combination to produce devastation. This combining of two groups may also be true of all emotional disturbances.

The first group is drawn from the pathological elements that feed all serious emotional disorders. These are all components that come under the umbrella of what I call *symbol sickness*.

In the sections that follow I shall discuss the highly specialized dynamics particularly characteristic of this sickness. These special dynamics are intimately connected to and often spring from sociological, political, philosophical, and religious forces comprising world cultures, particularly of the West.

Does this mean if a central substance from either group is missing, the disease will not be formed? The answer is yes!

Does this mean that only people who are sufficiently neurotic or psychotic can generate the disease? The answer is yes!

Does this mean that every anti-Semite is emotionally disturbed? The answer is yes!

Does this mean that considering the prevalence of the disease, our society worldwide produces great disturbance? The answer is yes!

Does this mean that we live largely in a neurotic and psychotic world? Unfortunately, the answer again is yes!

2 > SYMBOL SICKNESS

Anti-Semitism and all bigotry-oriented illnesses are what I have come to call *symbol sicknesses*. Phobias and ultimately perhaps all emotional illnesses are in large measure symbol sicknesses. Without some groundwork in understanding emotional illness, we cannot go on to understand this or any other emotional disturbance. Therefore, I have devised this schema that I call symbol sickness to provide that understanding in as little space as possible. *Symbol sickness*, though, also highlights those characteristics of mental disturbance particularly applicable to our problem.

Symbol usage virtually defines the so-called normal human condition. We use symbols to represent all objects in the world. We think, talk, relate, invent, calculate, create, and even feel through the use of representational symbols. We communicate how we feel to each other and about each other with symbols. Symbols like *love* and *hate* have themselves many derivatives such as *being in love* and *detest*, describing many subtleties, branching feelings and meanings, as well as count-less permutations and combinations. Symbols vary from the almost concrete—knife represents a cutting instrument—although there are variations here, too—to the most abstract: as in mathematical representations and formulations.

As we become more complex beings and become progressively free from instinctual dictates, symbols become even more important in our lives. This occurs as we are increasingly influenced by all kinds of cultural and hierarchical dictates. Representative symbols of wealth, power, prestige, morality, evil, notoriety, etc., become powerful and sometimes complex behavioral motivating forces.

Freud said, "Sometimes a cigar is a cigar." But for the most part cigars and their counterparts are much more than cigars and more than phallic symbols, too. The cigar (a relatively simple symbol) can connote a thumb (the short stub of a cigar), power, benevolence, arrogance, maleness, affluence, effeteness, etc. So it can also be seen from this over simplistic example that a symbol can have diverse and even antithetical representations. Mood and events sometimes alter the meaning of symbols.

Obviously the symbol takes on meaning relative to the culture or society as well as the individual's personal experience. The smell of a cigar is comforting to me—it reminds me of my father's most prosperous period. To my wife they smell awful and remind her of her father's impoverished business and hard times. It turns out that cigars put us both in mind of politicians, businessmen, gamblers, and "wise guys" (from her), old gnarled men and young men trying to look older and more important. Neither of us was reminded of Freud, who smoked more than twenty cigars a day. Several of my cigar-smoking colleagues thought of Freud at once. At first some people had thoughts of cigars as phallic symbols. Some people had rapid and many associative symbols come to mind, some did not.

Symbols have a capacity then to produce chain reactions of other symbols or inhibition or arrest of all other symbol formation. I believe both these possibilities are more characteristic of symbols than of the objects they represent. Thus, the word _cigar_ may bring on more reaction than the presence of an actual cigar. This is especially true of emotional reactions. "Cigars?— God save me from the stinking, disgusting things."

Obviously, the symbol and its original object can be separated. In fact, a considerable gap can be established. Sometimes this gap can be big enough so that the symbol goes on autonomously and the object that it originally represent has been effectively obliterated. This brings us to *symbol sickness*.

We must view symbol sickness as the major underlying and contributing psychological disablement making anti-Semitism and most other illnesses of this kind possible. Indeed, anti-Semitism is itself a major symbol sickness and gives us an opportunity to view symbol sickness closely through this particular syndrome we call anti-Semitism.

Another way to see this is to say that symbol sickness is the umbrella disturbance and makes possible and feeds all other neurotic and psychotic defense systems or disturbances. This also means that nearly all disturbances—projection, paranoia, rationalization, etc.—are components of symbol sickness and comprise symbol sickness.

But in this chapter I will describe the main and general characteristics of symbol sickness. Then I will go on to describe the particular defense mechanisms that provide fertile ground for culturally influenced dynamisms of anti-Semitism to take hold. Symbol sickness is in a way a bird's-eye view of neurosis. While we all suffer from it to some extent, the degree varies and is all-important.

Now let me list and briefly describe the main aspects of symbol sickness.

S. GAP

Perhaps the most striking aspect of symbol sickness is the removal of the symbol from the object it initially is there to represent.

We may say that this gap, let us call it the *S. gap*, is pathognomonic (absolutely characteristic of the pathology) of the disease. The gap varies in size, largely directly proportional to the intensity and depth of the pathological process.

Thus, *Jew* may represent a person; or the word or thought may conjure up and bring to mind a vast array of associations more or less related to a person or persons; or it may bring to mind an assortment of monstrous, revolting, enraged associations and feelings totally removed from person or persons and in fact operate as a conditioned reflex totally removed from human object symbol relationship. When the latter happens, the dehumanization of anyone who is recognized as a Jew is automatic and makes inhuman action plausible.

We can readily see then that in extreme cases—of which there are many—the original or representational object may be effectively and entirely obliterated. Even the gap no longer exists and the symbol is now completely autonomous.

MINIMAL SYMBOL AUTONOMY

In symbol sickness then, there is always a gap and it follows that there is always at least *minimal symbol autonomy*.

This minimal symbol autonomy simply means that the symbol not only is removed from the subject but at least in part from the central thinking process of the host. In effect, it is like a bullet that has left the gun and, no longer controlled by the gun, can ricochet all over the place.

Sometimes the gap is so large and the symbol has taken on meaning and feeling so removed from the object that autonomy is maximum. We now have a "free symbol" that brings on all kinds of feelings no longer requiring the original object. Thus, the word *Jew* may automatically bring on feelings of disgust, fear, and hatred. Here, complete separation from the host has taken place. Thus we now deal with a possible third characteristic of symbol sickness—fragmentation.

FRAGMENTATION

Once the process of removal from central self or autonomy takes place—the autonomous symbol is now fragmented off central control. This process tends to spread out and even become malignant. This means that other emotionally laden and emotionally reactive symbols slip off and out of control of the host's central, logic rendering self.

I believe that in the condition of schizophrenia we often see this process of fragmentation and the action of autonomous symbol centers at its height. That is why the victims seem like many people beset by many impulses, each coming from a different center, all of which lack binding integration. Indeed, I further believe that the secondary, florid symbols that characterize this particular disease (schizophrenia)—hallucinations and especially delusions—are an attempt to form a new central, logical system. This is an attempt to integrate the many autonomous fragments. Is it possible that major anti-Semitism, in which the disease has become the central focus of the anti-Semite's life, is the same process? Could this victim be using *Jew* and all it connotes to him as a central focusing symbol that will integrate all of his aberrant, fragmented symbols so as to provide a sense of self-identification, some kind of logic, however removed from reality and however distorted?

DISTORTION

Without application of central self, logic no longer applies. The symbol is now free to take on any and all grotesqueries however removed from truth or rationale.

If the symbol, in this case, *Jew*, has become an obsessive central focus (the central point for an attempted new, synthetic integration), the distortion will be greatest.

This is so because the new system devised must accommodate all of the individual's feelings, conflicts, terrors, and other distortions, however much they defy logic. Thus, *Jew* must account for all of the individual's problems, frustrations, injustices, limitations, rages, etc. Thus, *Jew* must be seen in the utmost distorted, illogical way as inner necessity dictates. This accounts for the fifth characteristic, which is itself a distortion.

MUTUALLY EXCLUSIVE SUPERLATIVES

The Jew is seen as:

- Moronic, brilliant.

- Sadistic, masochistic.

- All-powerful, weakling.

- Cosmopolitan, provincial.

- Cunning, naïve.

- Extraordinarily sensitive, calloused.

- Ruthlessy calculative, wildly impulsive.

- "Nigger-lovers," "worst bigots."

- Best lovers, worst lovers.

- Coarse and ill-mannered, polished sophiscates.

- Richest, poorest.

- Exquisitely sensitive, totally coarse.

- Artistic, tasteless.

- Child-lovers, child-killers.

- Money-lovers, intellectual snobs.

- Socially pushy, exclusively clannish.

- Most human, inhuman.

Since the symbol provides a foil on which to project one's own inner conflicts, ambivalence, and self-hate as well as the displacement from other symbols and objects, we can readily understand the need to see (and often also to react to) the same symbol as polarized opposites. Eventually we shall see that use of the symbol as an object of projection and displacement is extremely important in anti-Semitism.

Since inner conflicts (e.g., the need to be moral versus the urge to have free sex) are very powerful and tend to be seen in an utterly self-hating light or in a purely idealizing one, polarization usually takes place. This polarization makes for the necessity of superlative characteristics to project to (the Jews are the most intelligent, most primitive, most unethical) in order to encompass the conflicting extremes.

EMOTIONAL INVESTMENT

The superlatives and the projections also make for great emotional investment as well as difficulty in dislodgement.

This simply means that very strong feelings develop about the symbol as well as great reactivity to the symbol. The symbol tends to take on increasing importance, and this can and often does reach a state in which there is obsessional preoccupation with it.

In this connection it is interesting to note that people who are given to the use of superlatives and to black and white, highly polarized outlooks (he's all good or all bad; the greatest or the worst) tend to be more vulnerable to symbol sickness. They also almost invariably come to be fixed in their own beliefs and the exaggerations, however much these are divorced from reality.

This tendency also makes for greater isolation of the symbol from the central identifying self, making the application of logic difficult or even impossible.

Once these beliefs or emotional investments take place, they become increasingly difficult to dislodge. This is so because the symbol becomes one of the building blocks or even the very foundation of a new (however unreal) adjunct self-identification process. Ridding self of a distortion is threatening to (1) one's feelings of identification: the whole edifice may crumble; (2) to one's confidence in one's own judgment (3) to one's pride (for example, in being right); (4) to one's projective mechanisms. If a person can't project difficulties rising from inner conflicts to outside symbols, he or she is forced to take responsibility for his or her own difficulties. This new taking on of responsibility requires considerable maturity and represents a big step toward health.

The symbol becomes the object to which one's inner conflicts are projected. Thus, symbols of groups of people who differ from the main population stream, such as blacks, yellows, Jews, etc., become objects of conflict projections. These conflicts include areas involving sex, especially sexual prowess and gender identification; anger, especially self-hating rage and violence; moneymaking ability connected to the need for dedication to education and the postponement of gratification; the need to be masterful and at the same time the need to be universally loved, etc.

In projecting inner conflict to, let us say, Jews, what really happens is that Jews—the symbol—are assigned roles representing aspects of one's own conflicts. This is an attempt to work out painlessly the conflict or to live with it.

For example—let us say that Joe idealizes himself—sees himself as the brightest, craftiest, sexiest, etc., and also sees himself as greasy, loathsome, untrustworthy, impotent, etc. He assigns Jews both roles and sometimes only one role (as projected self-hate) and attempts to dissipate his feelings, especially anger, self-hate, and anxiety, through psychodrama involving Jews. Jew, the symbol, then takes on all of the necessary characteristics for Joe to play out his inner drama as that symbol becomes utterly divorced from Jew, the actual person. Thus we can readily see the need for distortion, exaggerated superlatives, tenacity of belief and great efforts exerted to promote and sustain the stereotype once the disease has taken hold.

The distortion is a direct offshoot of the confused notions about self and the attempts to clarify by seeing self in simple black-and-white terms.

The exaggerated superlatives stem from the self-idealizing process that itself is a reaction to low self-esteem and insecurity. Idealization is always extreme and falls from glory always produce extreme self-hate.

Tenacity in keeping irrational belief intact is due to the fear of self-confrontation and revelation of the truth as well as fear of conflictual feelings of being torn apart.

Therefore, it behooves the victim not only to sustain the projection at all cost but to continue to feed, extend, and strengthen the stereotype regardless of the illogic, lack of objectivity, and even the complete lunacy of the belief.

THE STEREOTYPE

This dedication to the distorted symbol, the stereotype, is a principal characteristic of symbol sickness.

The disturbed person uses any influence at all from the environment to strengthen, to support, and to augment his stereotypical thinking. He will seek out the most prejudicial elements to support his belief. He will do anything to further belief in the stereotype, including the fabrication of blatant lies.

If he needs to see the Jew as a passive and what he perceives as a feminine symbol, he will support castration of the Jew politically, socially, and economically. He will support the archetype of intellectual, nonassertive wimp even as he supports notions of ill-mannered, pushy, expansive aggressiveness.

His beliefs are then set by his internal needs and scraps and bits he feeds on supplied by his environment. If popular opinion feeds his distorted viewpoint, as is largely true in Jew hating, so much the better.

He is absolutely rigid in his belief, unmoved by fact or logic, and can become obsessive and even psychotic, as was the case with Hitler, who was really certifiable. That Hitler was not committed to an insane asylum tells us much about a population that shared his needs and viewpoint.

OBSESSION, CONTAGION, AND SUGGESTIBILITY

If a stricken individual has sufficient internal conflict so as to generate intolerable anxiety, a powerful diversion is sought after to deflect pain. If the diversion is condoned and even contributed, suggested and surreptitiously or blatantly approved and even praised by society, we then have fertile ground for obsession.

In these cases, the symbol becomes the central integrating focus and force in the individual's life I spoke of earlier.

It is at this point much more that a divisive force. It is now the very hub of self-identification and its identifying force increases geometrically as time goes on. Therefore, it behooves the victim to do everything possible to sustain the insane beliefs inherent in the disease. This includes, in bigotry, to contribute in any way possible to exaggerate already grossly distorted realities concerning the object of the prejudice. For example, in

Jew hating, the obsessed patient (let us call one a patient even if he is not in much-needed treatment) will join any force to deprive Jews of work and then curse Jews for shiftlessness and for their refusal to work for other people. In obsessed bigots this kind of double-bind—damned if you do, damned if you don't—fabrication is exceedingly common. This mechanism is also common in emotionally disturbed parents who project self-hate to their children.

Hysterical people, with very poor self-esteem, are extremely suggestible. They are desperate for simplistic explanation and solutions, especially for those they may find outside themselves. This makes them highly vulnerable to bigotry and especially to hate, which purports to solve their problems and is often sold by culturally condoned salesmen of bigotry.

Since low self-esteem, much internal conflict, and inner disturbance run rampant among us, great hordes of people are highly susceptible to serious symbol sickness.

This sows the seeds for pandemic infection. Hitler knew this and drew heavily on his own psychotic preoccupation to foster it in a large neurotic population. Just as Jew hating seemed to give him a pseudo sense of superior identification and integration, he used the latter on the masses. In promulgating Jew hating he made his people feel superior—that is, the masses—and he also integrated them into a pseudo whole; their commonality being their illness—hating Jews. This force for contagion made them easy to manipulate. An array of Jew haters can be wielded easily by a master Jew hater. Of course, the entire process becomes malignantly contagious in a society that either subtly or blatantly condones, praises, and even rewards its most diseased members.

And now what about pseudo feelings of superiority that are so often a major component of symbol sickness?

EXAGGERATED AND COMPULSIVE HIERARCHICAL STRIVING

Unfortunately, nearly all of us come to measure ourselves relative to other people and thus other people's status takes on high and highly distorted symbolic value. There are any number of constructs that abound, all of which lead to illusionary glory and to real self-hate and to deprecation of others.

There are ladders with various hierarchical rungs and various combination contained therein: looks, color, race, religion, profession and professional standing, familial standing, fraternal connections, intellectual standing, macho positioning, etc. Eventually nearly all areas of life are represented on a scale designating relative status.

The general effect of striving for status is the production of adversarial seesaw relating. "If you are down, I am up." This becomes the operative here.

Of course, this kind of society produces many symbols and much distortion and designated stereotyping as well as a great many people suffering from symbol sickness. Rhyme and reason go out the window. Blue eyes may be designated as better than dark eyes; tall better than short; Gentile better than Jew, etc.

The most likely victims are people who feel inadequate and also feel they must strive and at the same time are paralyzed in their endeavor to get ahead of the next fellow.

This does not prevent them from putting the next fellow down in their minds or through identification with any group that does this for them.

A powerful trend to achieve status in society's many hierarchical areas combined with great limitations produces frustration. Relief is attempted through the shortcut of bringing symbolic victims down to levels below one's own supposed level, thus raising oneself—at least in the imagination.

Exaggerated striving—without success—is often coupled with much exaggeration of symbolic representation of designated people, some as being very high and some as very low on the scale. Jews are often singled out as being both high and low, relative to the needs of the symbol sufferer. They are and have everything in all walks of life or they are and have nothing, making the symbol sufferer feel both put down and superior relative to Jews, the symbol.

In exaggerated hierarchical striving, self-pity and feeling abused and left out invariable lead to self-idealization and feelings of entitlement. These lead to further feelings of unjustified deprivation and undeserved lack of recognition. These "lacks" are easily projected to persons or groups who become symbolized as unjustified possessors of it all as well as deprivers. In extreme cases, where the vicious cycle has been going on for a long time, paranoia takes root and the symbolic depriver is often then seen as a deadly and dangerous enemy. Putting *them* down then becomes an act of justice, getting even, and raising oneself in the hierarchy, all at the same time.

CONFORMITY AND COMPLIANCE

Here, if severe enough, self-responsibility is unnecessary and the need for making decisions is obliterated. Dependency on symbolic authority in the form of demagogues, stars, popular opinion, and often just casual acquaintances dictates feelings, thoughts, values, and lifestyles. This dependency on various manifestations of authority is often the influence of parents during childhood continued into adulthood. This kind of immaturity is fostered by authoritarian cultures and is exploited and used politically.

But even the mildest conformity takes its toll on the would-be autonomous self. This is especially true in societies that value popularity and obsessive nationalism. Living without awareness, people learn whom and what to like and hate, to respect and to despise.

In many cases, symbols of authority are idealized and elevated to godlike status. This makes the dependent person feel more secure and less in need to grow up. It also provides a much-needed sense of belonging to an extended family, a privileged group. Through identification with the idealized leader and with what is seen as power, one's own self-idealization is fed and serves as compensation for poor self-esteem.

The suggestibility of people suffering in this way is extremely high. They can literally be sold on just about anything and especially by big lies involving extremes and superlatives. They view the latter as evidence of expertise and further authority. Gullibility is increased with loss of self and the ability to apply objective reality is lost also. (Hitler knew this and exploited it ruthlessly to further his ends. He understood that the bigger and more outrageous the lie, the more authoritative power it would contain for the compliant masses.)

Quick and thorough submission to the will of others is characteristic and as one's own feelings are blunted and obliterated.

Denial, passivity, and resignation are commonplace. These prevent reality from intruding and making independent evaluation and action possible. In this way, conformity is guaranteed to continue as are distortions applicable to object symbols.

AMBIVALENCE AND CONFLICT

In symbol sickness there is much fragmentation. There is little central autonomy. There are many board members—each screaming for recognition—and there is no chairman. Well-established values are missing. Priority is established by impulse rather than by design. Mixed feelings are numerous as well as potential for constant shifting.

In severe cases we are dealing with a person who lives in a chronic transitional state. He is between everything and anchored to nothing. Stereotypes offer the possibility of landmarks. Demagogues offer salvation from ambivalence and inner conflicting forces that produce constant anxiety and lack of direction.

In the desperate creation of a pseudo-self designed for synthetic integration and identification, the victim may repress and destroy all semblance of conscience. Right and wrong, ethical and moral equivocation no longer being operational saves him from having a castigating conscience—which he effectively obliterates. This saves him from conflict. Raising himself above moral issues, he may become a godlike, grandiose megalomaniac.

The combination of psychopathy (lack of conscience) and psychosis (megalomania) produces an individual devoid of empathy, sympathy, and compassion. Combined with intelligence, leadership and knowledge of a population not unlike himself and in search of authority, he becomes deadly, dangerous.

Obviously all cases are not this advanced and dangerous. Those that are may not be found in a vulnerable population and may appropriately find their way into a mental hospital.

But to any extent that symbol sickness exists, severe ambivalence and some vulnerability to gross distortion exists also as does a dearth of compassion.

ENVY

Envy plays such an important role in Jew hating that I feel it is necessary to explore it in some depth here.

Where hierarchical striving exists, it is not possible ever to eradicate this enormously self-corrosive and joy-killing human poison. The role of envy is enormous in all symbol sickness but especially in bigotry, even though it may sometimes be totally repressed and relegated to an unconscious level. Symbol sickness here involves the symbolic possessor and the symbolic dispossessed. In the mind of the victim, gross exaggeration always exists.

There are, of course, various degrees of envy and different stages as well. But the groundwork is always there in greater or lesser intensity. These precursors may be subtle and unconscious or blatant and conscious. Let us briefly look into these precursors first.

DEGREES OF ENVY

- The envious autodigestive victim always has exaggerated feelings of inadequacy, deprivation, impoverishment, powerlessness, and sometimes helplessness. These are largely based on poor self-esteem—may or may not be connected to some measure of reality— and nearly always derive from damaged relationships in early childhood. Everything owned by one's self is downgraded and deprecated.

- The victim always feels abused and entitled and believes that symbolic possessors unjustifiably have more through luck, manipulation, belonging to the "right" group, or through downright malevolence on their part. There is often an implication that possessors and the system that supports them are free of moral and ethical ties that bind underprivileged people. Envious people feel that they deserve everything they do not have and what they have is never enough to compensate for just desserts or what they should have.

- Projection is invariably present in envious people. Their emotional state of well-being is always out there in other people's hands. They are more interested in what other people have and have not than what they themselves own. Their moods are largely directed by what they think the status of these symbol people happens to be and thus these moods may fluctuate wildly. They believe the envied person has it all—everything! If they can establish a symbol (Jews) that always accounts for their state of misery, they may produce a synthetic state of relative stability and equilibrium. Hence, it behooves them to find steady objects of envy on whom to concentrate blame as well as sustained and chronic hate. This provides stability, meaning, focus, and relief of self-hate. It also removes the need for self-responsibility for one's own condition, making real change unnecessary and impossible.

- Their state of wretchedness and the better condition of the envied often have little connection to objective reality. Distortions about themselves and the elevated status of others abound. These illusions are largely the effect of self-pity—the source for the chronic abused reactions that are so common in people who envy others. Where self-pity has been present for a long time, helplessness and powerlessness give way to hopelessness and resignation. The feeling of being no-caste outcasts and hopelessness often leads to a sense of inner deadness.

- Inner deadness and hopelessness are relieved by rage at a privileged and envied symbol. Rage, often in the form of chronic repressed anger, is largely generated by illusionary perceptions of supposed injustices. These are magically ascribed to the hated symbol. This rage and the active process of envy itself give a sense of synthetic aliveness that needs constant fueling. These mechanisms provide reverberating vicious cycles, extrication from which becomes most difficult—hence, great resistance to reality occurs.

• This resistance to reality is characteristic of the disease (envy and Jew hating) and especially so in people in whom envy has become the central force of their character structures. When questioned, these victims say that they wish to own what you have but do not want to be what you are. This means in part that they want it all but don't want the work and the responsibility involved in getting it. Also, they want it (what they think you have) but want you out there in position so that they can continue to project their hatred to you and to sustain their rage and the envy process. This accounts in part for the ease of taking all that Jews own an even claiming Jewish accomplishments for themselves even as they keep the now impoverished Jew in mind as symbols of privilege and hatred so as to still sustain envy. Resistance to reality is actually resistance to giving up what is now felt as the core of identity, a raison d'etre, a focus of pseudo-integration, a source of aliveness, and at the same time an object of derision that makes for feelings of superiority. How can a person who at root feels inadequate, hopeless and empty give up what is felt as a major source of nourishment? How can an emotional infant take on responsibility for self required in adulthood? How can an incredibly self-castigating person utterly lacking in compassion face the explosive rage at self formerly directed at the envied symbol? Yet this is what is required initially if reality is ever to be contemplated.

• The promotion of hierarchical striving by society, the socioeconomic culture we live in must be viewed as an important precursor for the generation of envy. Possessions, statures through self-glorification and through notoriety are constantly promoted by the media. The implication is always there of a mythical Nirvana world whose portals only the privileged may pass through. We are made to believe and envy those of privilege who can escape the ordinary problems and tribulations of life. We are made to envy and emulate "stars" in all areas of our lives as we compete with and envy our neighbors and friends for their cars, odors, sexual attractiveness, prestige, children, health, popularity, and belonging to *right* groups of all kinds.

STAGES OF ENVY

Depending on the degree of symbol sickness, envy may go through various stages of progressive deterioration. These encompass from the mildest, imperceptible conditions to all-encompassing, blatant psychosis. In each stage, severity varies.

- Desiring to have something or things the other, envied person is *believed* to possess. This can be a mild wish or an overwhelming preoccupation. Even at this stage, self-hate can be intense and this may be converted to hatred of the envied person who is seen as the depriving enemy. Interestingly, as with all symbol sickness, paradoxes are common. Even as there is hatred for the other person, the desire to trade places may also exist. Commonly, however, at this stage the patient just wants to own things the other person is represented as having. Invariably the victim also has the feeling that what he or she does possess is second-rate and even worthless.

- In this second stage, especially in morbidly dependent people, there is a desire to have everything the other person is believed to have. I have seen cases in which the victim would actually like to trade places and be the other person. This desire often covers a deeply unconscious desire to meld with the other person so as to provide an adequate and more desirable self.

• This stage, which we may call the vindictive stage, is characterized by the desire for the envied person to own nothing—to be totally deprived. In effect, the hated self has been transferred to the other person and in the eradication of the other person; one's hated self is made to disappear. This dynamic goes on totally out of the awareness of the victim. Coupled with depersonalization, an effect characteristic of symbol sickness, which I will describe shortly, this stage can be dangerous to the object of envy. Fantasies of vindictive triumph in which envied people lose everything, even their lives, and the envier gets everything are common. Unfortunately, this can become a total preoccupation, a deep and all-encompassing psychosis, and we can, we know, translate fantasy into reality [Hitler].

• This is the invidious stage. It is an advanced stage in the illness (envy), even though it may occur early on along with the first stages. But it is always evidence of increased degeneration of constructive forces and tends to be obsessive, quickly dictating much motivation in the victim's life. In this stage the motive is to make others, especially the possessor, envious of the envier—oneself. This making others envious of ourselves is felt as ultimate vindictive satisfaction as well as a symbol of having arrived at privileged territory after all. Unfortunately, satisfaction, as with

most neurotic defenses, is short-lived and requires increasing fuel—in this case, more and more envy by
others. This is aided by imagined or real degradation
of the formerly envied and imagined elevation and
idealization and glorification of oneself. Depress
ingly, the media and especially the advertising world
contribute to this particularly insidious aspect of
the illness as it feeds hierarchical striving. Again and
again there are dramas designed to show that real
satisfaction in both achievement and acquisition of
status and things (auto, beauty, a youthful look, richness) comes through making others envious. Seeing
other people embarrassed or in pain and frustration
over their own limitations or impoverishment (own-
ing a lesser product) is seen as ultimate proof of ar-
rival and victory.

- *Jealousy*, from my point of view, is a degenerate stage
of envy. It may or may not coexist with the earlier
stages. In its lightest form the individual fears that
something will be taken away from her or him. In
malignant jealousy paranoia may be present, with
terror of attack and eradication by the individual
or group that was originally envied. In anti-Semitic
disorders it is commonplace to believe that Jews will
rob people of everything, especially status and even
their children or their lives. This stage is a logical end
point of envy since viewed through his or her eyes
the envious person believes that other people must
envy him or her, too. If he wishes totally to deplete
or annihilate the other person, he is vulnerable to
the belief that the "other" wants to hurt him. This
also provides rationale and justification for his quite
irrational feelings and actions.

THE CORROSIVE EFFECTS OF ENVY

The corrosive effects of envy on self have in large part manifested themselves in our discussion so far. Now let me summarize and add a few others.

- Inner peace is not possible. It is replaced by a restless, anxious, ever ongoing, disheartened, cynical disgruntlement.

- Ownership of real assets, including money, objects, power, talent, friendships, accomplishments, etc., never really takes place. All that one owns is denigrated and compared to envied ideals, never accruing to a sense of betterment. Instead, all is used as evidence to demonstrate impoverishment relative to "what could have been" and to what others seemingly have.

- Inability to experience joy through any satisfaction at all perhaps represents the biggest loss. Of course, participation in other people's joy and achievements (often even in one's own children) is precluded. Unfortunately, envious people make excellent foul-weather friends, reveling in others' miseries.

- Depletion of energy, will, hope, responsibility, focus, and motivation prevent the use and development of one's own resources and preclude creative output or satisfaction. Inner deadness, dulling of feelings, and still more loss of self-esteem are characteristic.

- Personal relationships are disturbed and in lieu of joy being with other people produces still more envy. Most relationships for envious people are competitive adversarial ones. The main dynamic is making sure that the other person never gets ahead of oneself. Claims on others and on fate, God, and the world generally, abound. When these claims are thwarted, abused reactions and self-pity are generated. Other people are viewed as enemies and chronic repressed anger pushes aside all other emotions. The corrosive effect makes the envious person vulnerable to still more envy ("everyone is happier than me"). This sustains vicious cycles. Envy demands relief. Hatred of the symbolic possessor provides synthetic relief in the form of irrational rage that never compensates for increasing feelings of inner deadness. Inner deadness is fed by the externalizing effects of envy. The fact is that the sick individual's fate is always in other people's hands—the person whom he envies—rather than his own. This externalizing effect, removing one's center from one's inner self is a major life tragedy.

ALIENATION FROM FEELINGS, DEHUMANIZATION, AND DEPERSONALIZATION

The sum total of symbol sickness in all forms results in removal from and deadening of feelings. Near automaton states—going through motions—are common.

Judgment born of a human value system based on feelings is aberrated and missing. Range of feelings (different feelings) and intensity of feelings are constricted and weak.

In effect, a dehumanization process has taken place and a person is replaced by a thinking robot. The robot suffers from lack of judgment ordinarily rooted in the conscience, which makes us discern right from wrong through identification with others whom we feel for. Anxiety generated from wrongdoing is attenuated.

Applied to others, the thinking machine may think of them not as people but as dehumanized, depersonalized symbol objects, and may act accordingly. This means that empathy, sympathy, identification, and compassion may be attenuated, quite dilute, and even dead.

This removal of feelings from judgment and action coupled with high suggestibility and the habit of unquestioningly responding to authority with utter compliance makes even the most monstrous actions possible.

But, being human, there may still be a craving for feeling—an urge to mitigate deadness in some way, to come to life.

Unfortunately, the easiest path here is perverse. Sadism—vicariously living through other's feelings, especially through pain engendered by the robot like person—becomes the path of least resistance.

Pain and power are strong stimulants. They can also be used in the service of hierarchical striving. They momentarily satisfy the attack on deadness. When they fail, still more pain is inflicted, and if necessary, murder—which momentarily satisfies the need for power. Thus sadism becomes a common adjunct of the condition.

It must be remembered that alienation is fed by all other manifestations of symbol sickness and also nourishes all of its tributaries. Therefore, the effect on personality is highly malignant and metastatic, affecting all areas of behavior.

Where alienation and conscience deadening exist to any extent, means come to justify ends and distortions and lies replace reality as needed. This is possible because feelings and conscience are not adequate to raise objections to either distortions or to gross untruths, which quite easily become tools in the service of all kinds of insane goals.

In this way, it is not unusual for populations of alienated people to construct subcultures that are utterly bizarre, psychotic systems—the values of which are grossly removed from any semblance of civilized norms. This in large part accounts for Hitler's Germany—the existence of a Wagnerian symbol sickness construct—a psychotic sociopathic, floridly monstrous, operatic, death-oriented, megalomaniac, paranoid world. Unfortunately, this existed on a national basis, but it can also take place on an international basis and often takes place in fragments of small cults throughout the world, all of which practice forms of the same insanity.

UNCONSCIOUSNESS

Unconsciousness is one of the most striking features of symbol sickness.

The victim may be more or less aware of the existence of his/her disturbance. But it is not unusual for the illness to go on totally out of awareness. Thus, the severely envious person may swear that he/she is not envious at all. The anti-Semite may have no awareness of his/her feelings about Jews but may always act in a hostile fashion to them.

Unconsciousness may go on despite blatant evidence and awareness by other people. A process of keeping oneself out of awareness is necessary so that self-idealization may continue to flourish. It also takes place so that the illness and its particular emotional economy is guaranteed to go on unthreatened and unabated. The victim may know how he or she feels about Jews but is not aware that his or her feelings and actions are at all related to personal illness. One aids this process by rationalization—"Doesn't everyone feel that way?" or "I detest them because they are in fact detestable. Therefore I am just being realistic." One's symbol sickness easily remains mysterious when it is supported by an entire society that suffers from the same disease. "What's all this fuss about Jews anyway?" is another common comment.

Denial and compartmentalization are also common mechanisms used in the service of unconsciousness.

"Isn't it natural to want to be with your own kind?"

"Some of my best friends are Jews."

"You are not one of them. You are more like us. You are Jewish but not really a Jew."

Of course, to the extent that depersonalization (of the hated person) has taken place, it is so much easier to hate—without being aware that it is people whom one is hating, after all.

It is not unusual for symbol sickness victims to like individuals and to hate the symbol. Thus the anti-Semite may in some cases work and socialize with people who are Jewish and keep himself from facing it or even knowing it while he hates *them*— the Jews out there. Anti-Semites are often genuinely shocked when confronted with the Jewish identification of their confreres. The combination of confrontation with humanization and Jewishness is too much for them to deal with.

But in this connection, the all-important fact is that people suffering from symbol sickness don't know it. Even when they are aware of something being amiss in their perceptions, the dynamics involved completely elude them and exert their enormous influence on a totally unconscious level.

Victims of the disturbance are not cognizant of the dynamics feeding their symptoms, and confused, sick rationalization usually convinces them of the logic of their perceptions and judgments, even when full consciousness is present.

3 > RAGE AND INTENSITY

Symbol sickness may be mild and subtle or blatant and severe. It always produces neurotic elements and often at least some psychotic elements, too. In some states psychosis is paramount and removal from reality is pronounced. Psychopathy—deadening and even total annihilation of conscience and moral machinery—may take place. This psychopathy may combine with psychosis and produce an extremely dangerous, potentially destructive, and even violent creature, which I will discuss later on in the book.

Usually, all elements that I discussed are present. Some elements exist in greater strength than others. Various combinations may result in different symptoms, but vulnerability to cultural influences is always present, making bigotry commonplace.

In symbol sickness, reality has a difficult and even desperate time surviving. Objectivity, rationale, and logic are usually surrendered to inner needs and outside influence. Degree of surrender determines the extent of dehumanization, loss of spontaneity, and automatonlike behavior. Inconsistencies, blatant lies, confusion, and paradoxes abound. Judgment is aberrated and morality and ethnical considerations give way to narcissistic pre-occupation. Self-glorification destroys the value of human goodness. The difference between right and wrong in human issues is obliterated. Everything, however monstrous, becomes possible.

Once symbol sickness becomes malignant, vast generalization takes place. Individual identities are wiped out. The Jew becomes "one of them." The symbol applies to the entire group and to any and all of its members despite sick rationalizations like—"He's a Jew but he's different." In the mind of the symbol sufferer there are never any real differences between the individuals. Generalizations abound and dehumanization is often complete.

PART II

4 > CULTURAL INFLUENCES

What is it in our culture or what is it about Jews that makes them the most common object and symbol of this sickness?
Why are they singled out this way
Why is this particular manifestation of symbol sickness—Jew hating—so prevalent?
Why is it so persistent?
Why is it so intense—making possible severe and psychotic, sociopathic, criminal acting out, and sadistic murder?
How does the Jew come to be the leading recipient of the influences of symbol sickness described in the last section and the cultural influences I shall presently describe?
The cultural socioreligious dynamics described in no way reflect on the philosophy or values of real religious beliefs. This is a case in which religious beliefs have been neurotically and for the most part unconsciously perverted by symbol sickness. In this perversion an even more malignant symbol sickness has been created.

Please note that in the following pages I speak of dynamics applicable only to sick people suffering from Jew hating and not to their coreligionists who do not suffer this way!

Every Jew hater suffers from his own combination of these dynamics, some of them having greater or weaker influences in individual cases.

These poisonous vectors, present in different degrees, tend to feed each other and to overlap.

5 > JESUS WAS A JEW AND THE SPLIT DEVICE

J esus was a Jew! This belief (be it a historical fact or not) is, I believe, probably the single and most significant factor in the explosion of the disease. Hatred of Jews predated Jesus, but metastatic spread had not yet taken place.

Interestingly, those of us who are fully conscious of this belief are the least affected by it. But a vast number of us are not conscious of it. The Jewish origin of Jesus is largely repressed and relegated to the unconscious.

As with other psychic tragedies, the unconscious forces are the ones that confuse, terrify, dictate, and destroy. Unconsciousness removes sick dictates from the possibility of confrontation and constructive change.

The Jews are felt to be god producers and Jesus is the foremost of the gods. There are others, but we will talk about them later.

But Jesus is not and was not the God of the Jews. In fact, is is inconceivable to them that people can accept a man (a Jew) as God—this despite messianic desires and predictions.

This, too, was known and largely relegated to the anti-Semite's unconscious—this making of gods and saints for other people to believe in—people who will never, despite total loyalty, ever be, like the Jews, related to Him by blood. Does this create envy and hate and a symbol for the projection of self-hate born of lack of God connections? Yes! But even more important, is it possible that it creates a symbol for displacement, displacement of unconscious hatred of God to Jews, who produced Him? To make matters worse, these envied and hated God producers are always present as a reminder of Him, Jesus, and His dictates—all of which they seemingly escape, producing a double insult. Let me explain.

An interesting split takes place here, one that is quite common in symbol sickness. I said earlier that it is not unusual to like the person and despise the symbol. Variations of this dynamic occur constantly. Sometimes this applies to one person as person and symbol; sometimes the person is liked and a relative, seen as an extension of that person but safely removed from the liked person, is disliked, even though the despised relative may be virtually unknown. This kind of split makes ambivalent feelings easier to bear and prevents the feeling of being pulled apart by internal conflict. It also removes fear of vengeance by the liked person, especially if that person is viewed as being powerful and capable of inflicting punishment.

Thus, in keeping with the possibility I suggest, Jesus is loved for so much that is lovable in Him. Is it possible that what is hated about Him and terrifying is displaced to His relatives and producers—the Jews? This is made easy by several factors:

- Since the Jews do not believe in His divinity, their connection to Him is invalidated and therefore they are safe to victimize. He will not mind.

- Since they are not connected to His Godly status, unlike Jesus Himself, they are too weak to exact vengeance.

- They are relatively clannish, isolated, mysterious people, and it is much easier to displace and project to the unknown. There are relatively few facts born of familiarity to allow reality to interfere with need.

- By isolating them, in actuality and mind, setting them apart makes it safer to displace hatred without the danger of generating self-hate through hating one's own confrere or coreligionist.

- The secret desire to please a God who could not convince His own relatives that He was God, to punish them for Him, is attractive. The reality that Jesus Himself never gave up His own being a Jew remains well hidden in the unconscious. This serves as a cover-up of the real truth—the terrifying hatred of Jesus Himself.

- The "fact" (a misbegotten belief) that the Jews do not suffer from impositions and constrictions visited upon believers by the Jewish Jesus persists. Envy of this envisioned freedom is enormous and we will talk about it later.

- In displacing hatred to the nonbeliever there is reinforcement of the fact of their own belief. The greater their own need to rebel and the greater their own disbelief, the more hatred takes place of Jesus, necessitating more displacement to his originators. This provides an outlet for hatred even as it reinforces one's belief and restores an illusion of being safely identified with God after all.

6 > WHAT IS HATED AND DISPLACED?

The imposition of a conscience! The knowledge and performance of right and wrong! The generation of guilt relative to ethical considerations and people relating! The notion, influence, and performance relative to moral equivocation!

The inhibitions, prohibitions, and limitations imposed by conscience, preventing free, blatant acting out in every area of life.

These include the freedom to exercise pure rage, revenge, murder, rape, torture, etc.

Yes, Jesus is hated for insisting on compassion, love, forgiveness, and consideration of others. These get in the way of primitive and self-satisfying urges of all kinds, characteristic of people suffering from symbol sickness and stunted emotional social development.

He is hated for insisting on sexual restrictions and standing in the way of what has eventually been labeled as perverse. This in large measure accounts for the psychotic belief in the exotic and perverse sexual practices of Jews. In this case, a combination of displacement and projection takes place. The would-be pervert hates Jesus for standing in his way of satisfaction. Fearing Jesus and his own ambivalence, he displaces this hatred to the Jew. He also projects his own desire for perversion and the self-hate this produces to the Jew. He sees the Jew as the pervert, fallen from grace, and himself safe in the love of his God. This goes on even as he secretly envies the Jew for freedom that he believes the Jew has in taking pleasure in his perversion.

Eventually, Jews are hated for all inner coercions and contracts one may have with oneself as well as outer coercions. These may include constrictions born of an overwhelming, tyrannical, pleasure-depriving conscience that has no real connection to Christ, church, or religion at all. Thus, a perfectionist's inability to have joy and the self-hate produced by the lack of perfection and failed expectations may easily be swept along in the prohibitions ascribed to that conscience-giving Jewish part of Jesus—now seen as exclusively residing in Gentiles while Jews are seen as *free*.

Peculiarly, constructive forces such as cooperative relating, brotherly love, consideration for others, the pleasures derived from the practice of goodness, etc., may be lumped together with moral and ethical dictums and therefore may also be seen as conscience producers of constriction and guilt.

This is especially true of people who suffer from chronic repressed anger. Anything that seems to stand in the way of total potentially destructive "letting go" is secretly ascribes to the hated part of Jesus and consciously felt as hatred for the Jew, even though the cause of the hatred is buried in the unconscious.

I believe that chronic rage, born of feelings of inadequacy and helplessness, having roots in early childhood, combined with unconscious linkage and splits in feelings about Jesus, the Jew, produces many members for notorious hate organizations.

Some of these people who commit the worst atrocities do so in order to strike back at an overwhelming tyrannical conscience that he made them impotent automatons.

Many members of these hate groups in becoming Jew killers are actually conscience killers. The Jew is hated for being a conscience giver rather than a Christ killer. Even as they kill the hated conscience-giving part of Jesus symbolized by the Jew, they brag about love for Jesus and Christian brotherhood. In effect, they can accept and love Jesus if they symbolically separate Him from what they perceive as His conscience-giving tyranny. Killing Jews becomes to them further proof of Christian fidelity and solidarity.

This superego part of Christ attributed to Jews in the anti-Jewish unconscious makes the Jew the primitive mother of Christ and conscience. The Jewish mother is seen as giving, but she and the Jews as collective mother through conscience are also seen as crushing manhood. (Manhood is felt as freedom from impulse control and is confused with sexual abandon, aggression, and cruelty practiced without conscience or guilt.) This contributes to homophobia and to homophobic displacement to Jews and is a major dynamic in understanding violence directed at Jews which I will discuss later.

In this connection, the Jews are hated for contributing Christ to the world (as moral constriction—conscience) rather than for the fiction that they are Christ killers.

In fact, I believe that rabid anti-Semites who have convinced themselves of the historical delusion that Jews killed Christ unconsciously really admire and envy them for doing so. This follows inasmuch as the Jews have killed off the real object of their hatred—Christ, the conscience giver. They also are secretly grateful to the Jew for providing them with a symbol to which they can displace their hatred. Hating Jesus directly is terrifying indeed and threatens overwhelming guilt, unbearable self-hate, and eternal damnation. Calling Jews "Christ killers" supports shaky identifications with Jesus and even more so with His teachings. This helps convince the victim that as the Jews killed Christ, the hater of Jews loves Christ. I believe that on an unconscious level the anti-Semite's hatred of Christ is directly proportional to the belief in the fiction of Jewish deicide. The louder the cry of "Christ killer," the greater the effort at burying the unthinkable—hatred of Him. Here again I speak of Christ, the ethics giver, the conscience and morality giver, who disseminated ethical dictums to which none of the Jews were subject (in the anti-Semite's mind) before the advent of Christ.

Then what does Christ killer really mean? What unconscious message is given with that *curse*? Is it possible that on seeing the Jew as Christ killer, the Jew is actually admired and even envied for the misbelief that he killed Christ? Would the screamer, "Christ killer," really like to scream, "I envy you for doing it and really would have liked to do it myself."

Is the Jew hated for killing Christ or is he really hated for producing Christ and for being the god giver? Here again the anti-Semite responds to hatred of humane restriction of any kind even as he blames the Jew for all kinds of licentious behavior.

To the anti-Semite the crucifix, of which I shall soon say more, inevitably becomes a symbol and reminder of Jewish guilt. But on a deeper unconscious level it is a reminder of the Jew as progenitor of Jesus and his killer also.

My own thoughts about anti-Semitism and Jewish conscience giving through Christ and eventually through Christianity started during World War II. I was fairly certain that other people must have come to the same obvious conclusions regarding this dynamic. But I had no idea that Friedrich Nietzsche, the German philosopher, was one of these people and had predated me by many years.

My friend, Dr. Marvin Weitz, a superb historian, enlightened me several years ago (1984). In a particularly vitriolic, anti-

Semitic diatribe reminiscent of his latter-day admirer, Adolf Hitler, Nietzsche vents his hatred. He blames the Jews for insidiously fostering conscience and compassion inside the world through Christ and Christianity. He says that they distorted the use of the (German) word *gut* (good) as part of their plot. *Gut* or good originally meant, he says, war, glory, aggression, conquest, and all this is *gut* and natural to man. The Jews perverted *gut* to mean compassion, peace, moral equivocation, humility—all that is unnatural and stultifying and in effect castrating, especially to supermen striving, a justification that Hitler would use years later. Small wonder, Nietzsche became a source of philosophical delight to Hitler and to his Jew hating. Of course, Jewish morality, through Christ and Christianity, stood in the way of German supermen's ruthless glory-seeking aspirations. To both Nietzsche and other anti-Jewish sufferers, Jews are often seen as castrators rather than circumcisers.

7 > RIGHT AND WRONG AND THE EMBARRASSMENT OF CONSCIENCE

Unfortunately, we still live in a highly adversarial, competitive, and narcissism-producing world.

The "hooray for me, hell with you" psychology is prevalent. It produces a mass of mixed values, confused feelings, and hypocritical moves.

Narcissism and adversarial/competitive relating largely produces a system antithetical to the teachings of Jesus. His philosophy is the very antithesis of sociopathic, self-serving, hierarchical striving.

The attempt to reconcile cultural dictates that define success and cultural values born of Jesus and his teachings is virtually impossible. Definitions and lines separating right from wrong become more difficult and murkier with each generation.

Much current law is devoted to what one can do and get away with even though it is ethically and morally wrong and would be condemned by Jesus. More and more, there is less and less difference between those who play the game by the

law and those who play the game outside the law because in-
terpretation of the law is used for personal success rather than
for moral good.

So this is a world in which some television ministers preach-
ing for the sake of the poor go home to mansions in chauf-
feured limousines. Church-going (and temple-going) faithful
hire lawyers to save themselves from white-collar crime pros-
ecution. Without belaboring the point, sociopathy and Jesus
both prevail and reconciliation of the two is hypocritical and
impossible—one gets in the way of the other.

For the anti-Semite, the Jew helps him to compartmentalize
and live in both worlds at the same time and to deal with the
embarrassment of conscience and ensuing anxiety.

The Jew is seen as the purveyor of greed personified and
becomes the object of projected guilt and self-hate. He also
becomes the object of the (again split) rage felt at Jesus for
standing in the way of pure greed and ruthless disregard for
one's fellows. And so again, even as pure love is expressed for
Jesus, hatred is displaced to the Jew. The unconscious belief
persists that before Jesus the Jews kept the tyranny of the Bible
to themselves.

Out of the split a simple equation is born: The more you
love Jesus, the more you hate the Jews. The more you love
Him, the more you love right over wrong. The love of right
gets in the way of enjoyable wrong and the uncensored process of practicing pure self-serving greed to the exclusion of
ethical consideration of others. This again produces hate for
Jesus, which is projected to the Jews. This process completes a
vicious cycle guaranteeing the continued life of the equation.

Interestingly, some of the worst pogroms have taken
place on Christian holidays, so much so that Jews in Europe anticipated these holidays with dread. Anti-Semites,

through brutalization of Jews, felt that they demonstrated their religious fervor and gave evidence of loyalty to Christ this way.

With enough alienation and depersonalization of object and enough of splitting displacement and projection of hate, a fertile ground for murder is prepared. We will soon discuss the detonating devices: intense fear and gender confusion that produce this kind of possibility.

8 > SIGN OF THE CROSS

W hy is the crucifixion of the most powerful and ubiquitous of religious symbols? I believe it is largely because we can all identify with Christ's suffering. Martyrdom, through self-sacrifice, elicits a powerful response of empathy and sympathy for the inevitable suffering inherent in the human condition. People will crusade and kill in the name of the martyr and to support glory through martyrdom.

But for the anti-Semite, the unconscious meaning of the crucifixion can be grossly aberrated and responses can be enormously exaggerated.

First it must be pointed out that the anti-Semite is not a good Christian! Whatever his image of himself may be, in fact human emotions like compassion and empathy are alien to him. He can be relatively and even completetly oblivious to the suffering of others due to his extreme alienation from feelings. He can also feel coerced and deeply annoyed by what he perceives as manipulation through the attempt to engender guilt.

He seldom sees suffering for the sake of others as worthwhile. Self-sacrifice is a concept far removed from people suffering from impaired self-esteem and compensatory self-inflation, self-preoccupation, and narcissism.

And yet, so common in the double-think and double-feel world of the severe symbol sickness sufferer, that he may be moved by Christ's suffering and martyrdom. Being moved and feeling guilty are not welcome feelings to the safely anesthetized alienated person. Therefore, even as he is moved, he is also annoyed by this aspect of the Jewish-born Christ. He is also often annoyed by reminders of Jewish suffering and especially the Holocaust—in this way a six-million-time reminder of Christ's death throught the death of His kinfolk.

Then what do I believe the crucifixion means to the anti-Semite?—and I speak here of deep unconscious meaning.

Largely, he feels it as a weapon, as a manipulative tool directed at him and designed to produce discomfort for him.

But he sees it as something else, too. For him it represents contemptuous feminine submission that plays an important role in his gender confusion, which I will soon discuss. In his confused world, though—even as he sees crucifixion as surrender and submission—he also sees martyrdom as a powerful manipulative tool and also as the epitome of attaining glory. Thus, once again he is confusedly ambivalent—enjoying hating Christ for His glory and power and despising Him for what simplistically seems to him to be His passive submission on the cross. He displaces this embarrassing and feared hatred to Jews.

This is made easier because the Jews also have been crucified through the centuries and have been gloriously martyred and have, like Christ, risen again through their survival and have also produced guilt. The Jews, too, have been submissive. And through these interpretations the Jews are also again seen as being close to Jesus both through blood and a history of persecution and rebirth and survival. Thus, once again they are envied and despised.

Unfortunately, the crucifix is also a reminder of Jewish guilt—of having killed the Lord. Even as it reminds the Jew hater of this event, as I discussed earlier, it stirs admiration, envy, and consequent guilt for that admiration of the people who are delusionally believed to have killed the hated symbol of a repressive conscience.

9 > A UNIQUE SOURCE OF ENVY AND ITS COMPLICATIONS

There are many distortions that provide a rationale for envy, and we will continue to discuss some of them as we go along, but in connection with what I have just said, there is a strange and unique source that I want to mention briefly now and that leads to peculiar complications.

I speak of Jews as the blood relatives of Jesus. The Jews are secretly seen as the real brothers, sisters, cousins, and children of Jesus, and this without effort on their part. This confers connection to divinity without struggle or loss of freedom born of moral Christian doctrines; it is simply there as a birthright.

The anti-Semite sees himself as never attaining blood relationship despite self-sacrifice and submission to what is seen as the will of God. Symbolic connection through any means of communion is felt as inferior to real family (genetic) connection. At best, the Christian relative is seen as a foster child.

To some victims of the disease, especially megalomaniacs, this connection, despite ambivalent hatred, takes on exaggerated importance. The connection that is lacking from their point of view and that Jews own as a natural birthright confers nobility and security. The latter two are highly prized, where self-hate, inadequacy, and the drive for compensating grandiosity are of major magnitude.

But as is so often true of the split and mutual exclusive thinking of symbol sickness victims, a peculiar split takes place here, too. Even as the Jew is envied and hated for his believed relationship to the Lord, he is despised for reminding the anti-Semite of the morality of Jesus.

If Jesus was a Jew, then He was also a mortal. His morality may be viewed as a temporary and necessary aberration however it is rationalized by such beliefs as the Virgin birth. The self-deluding, self-hating anti-Semite does not have the enormous inner strength and self-certitude necessary for faith and trust to take over. He is in fact highly vulnerable to all kinds of ambivalent doubts. The Jewish connection provides embarrassing assaults on the belief in Jesus' divinity. In so doing, the Jew is felt as the agent of confusion, self-doubt, and the source of having been possibly duped.

10 > THE CHOSEN PEOPLE AND
THE "LESSER GODS"

To the anti-Semite, the Jews were not chosen by God to have a covenant with Him. Consistent with their envy of Jews as being related to God, they believe the Jews manufactured God.

In other words, the Jews were some how chosen to produce God and, as Nietzsche proposed, to promulgate their ethical beliefs through His Son on the general population.

But to the anti-Semitic unconscious the Jews were also chosen to produce the lesser gods—the gods who affect Western civilization and indeed the world more than all other gods or people ever have.

Through God and the lesser gods, the Jewish effect on the world is seen and felt as being totally out of proportion to their small numbers. More important, even as they are despised and vilified, they are seen as accruing enormous glory and for this the anti-Semite's envy knows no bounds. Glory is seen by symbol-sickness sufferers as the pinnacle reward of hierarchical suffering. It is seen as the answer to all problems and the only way, a kind of magical way, to transcend death. The Jewish God brings glory—Jesus and the lesser gods and even Jews who merely do well in areas dominated by the lesser gods bring glory.

But the anti-Semite does not see this glory as accruing to the nation or to the general population. He sees it as Jewish glory, a separate glory that takes glory and potential success away from himself and his own non-Jewish people. He is demeaned by Jewish glory. He feels unduly influenced by it. He says, "Jews are everywhere," "Wherever you look there are Jews," "They control everything: banking, stock market, politics, theater, universities, everything." He reacts by forming clubs that keep Jews out. He attempts to ghettoize Jews as much as possible. He attempts to ascribe Jewish glory to knavery, lying, manipulation, clannishness, and even worldwide cabals that exclude non-Jews from positions of power. He projects his own anti-Jewish discrimination and sees the Jew as the self-isolating discriminator.

He may not know the "lesser gods" or he may have only an unconscious trace of awareness of them. But he feels the Jews as "special" and related to them or to privilege and to God even whenever a Jewish child does well in school or a Jew succeeds in any area of endeavor.

Who are the "lesser gods?" They are not messiahs or false messiahs, but they, too, are people—people who have succeeded beyond ordinary success to influence the population of the world and how it perceives itself and the universe. There are many, but to the anti-Semite a few stand out and to many delusioned people seem to be the real connections to God and create the basis for envy in various areas.

And what about Jewish success? It is not privileged success or genetic success. It is largely the result of persecution and ostracism. Jews had to learn to develop intellectual ability and were forced to learn about the value of the postponement of gratification. Jews have known since time immemorial that gratification would often not be possible for generations of progeny in a world in which they were chased from place to place. I shall talk more about postponement of gratification later on.

To Jew haters the lesser gods are Albert Einstein, Karl Marx, and Sigmund Freud and their disciples and the many Jewish Nobel Prize winners and other notable contributors to society as well.

These people and their influence on science, politics, economics, and psychological perception is enormous. How much it is connected to their Jewishness is a largely unanswerable theoretical question. But to the anti-Semite their success is due to being Jewish, to being chosen, to being privileged, to being part of a secret and sleazy cabal.

It can be argued that many anti-Semites don't know who these people are, let alone that they were Jewish. The disease metastasizes by traveling from anti-Semitic people who do know them as Jewish to people who don't. In the end, it is not important that these people are Jewish, so long as people of influence know this and use this in their hatred of Jews. Indeed Karl Marx was a virulent anti-Semite himself. That hatred will be passed on to others regardless of whether the fact of Jewishness is passed on or not. This chain reaction succeeds as long as the recipient is neurotic enough to make use of this contagious hatred to augment his/her own anti-Semitism.

11 > FEAR OF THE "TRUE" MESSIAH

There are those anti-Semites who have particularly great doubts about the validity of Jesus as the true messiah. This is especially true of people who actually have very little faith but who nevertheless idealize themselves as Christians. What if they had been wrong?

If we live by Judeo-Christian principles, then the Jews are the incontrovertible originators of it all and they are still waiting—for the true messiah. Jesus was a Jew, and the Jews say He is not *The One*! What if they are right? What if the Jews have been right all along? If the messiah is still to come, what is the relationship between the Jewish "true messiah" and the people who have not believed in Him?

What about the feelings of their God (whom they believe to be the one true God) about those who have persecuted the people who have believed and still do believe in Him? Aren't the Jews the chosen people? Chosen for what? Not to be especially His but to bring God's word and ways to all of His people. This is really how the Jews see themselves. Anti-Semites generally see the Jews as being unfairly, yet specially, chosen and privileged. What will happen to those people who have inadvertently chosen the wrong one and persecuted His true chosen messengers?

The anti-Semite is invariably paranoid. He lives in a state of terror even though this aspect of this symbol sickness may not always be apparent. He thinks in terms of vengeance—vengeance against others for falsely believed wrongdoings against himself. He believes others seek vengeance against him for supposed transgressions and guilt—real and imagined—that he has committed. He is often a purist, quite confused about the limits of the human condition, and therefore he may suffer much guilt from a belief in multitudinous sins. Who will punish him for his sins? Will it be the same God who through His messengers and His faithful, has produced the very conscience that has terrorized him? If there is a Jewish God, what punishment will He inflict for all the anti-Semite's transgressions, real and imagined? Will it be equal to the total of Jewish suffering through the ages? Will it be an eye for an eye? Will it be the equivalent of what that God did to the Egyptians and other nonbelievers in pre-Christ days?

Fear generates hate—especially of the object that generates fear as well as of objects connected to that object or to any object to which projection or displacement is easy.

The anti-Semite assumes that he is hated by the Jew at least as much as he hates the Jew. He must keep the Jew powerless and in sight at all times and if possible obliterate him because this secretive creature of secret cabals may have special powers, powers derivative of the God of the Old Testament. If he is very sick and preoccupied with Jew hating, the Jew hater may believe that all Jewish activity is directed against him and his and may one day culminate in vengeance by the Jewish God.

Better to destroy the enemy before he can inflict his insidious damage!

Attacks of doubt about the deity and religious beliefs will often exaggerate self-doubt generally, internal conflict, and painful anxiety. These require a symbol object to use for projection. The vicious cycle thus is repeated again and again, often with increasingly bizarre rationale and venom.

Jews warn against graven images. God is not visualized. There are Tzaddiks or wise compassionate men and *just* men (who are unknown to themselves and to others) in whose existence reside human goodness and the essence of the conscience of the species. There are no saints, Jews believe. There is no cult of name. Moses is not worshipped. He was a messenger and a leader and a man. He was in no way godlike. There is no picture of Him, really. Interestingly, Jews do not see God as perfect. They will argue with God, fearing no repercussions because they do see him as compassionate—usually.

The amorphous Jewish God flies in the face of belief in man as a God or God in man's image. The longing for a messiah, a savior, is a way of keeping hope alive. It is more a symbol and a process than a belief in fruition of the process for most Jews. This disbelief in a man's ability to be God, godlike, or to create a God-image—particularly one that resembles man or the human condition—demands humility. Jews are humiliated, I believe, because their belief in an amorphous God—one whose name shall not even be uttered—prevents self-glorifying idealization. It simply gets in the way of believing that God is one of us—a person—and therefore we are godlike. Jews believe that God is great but have no idea what he looks like. Humiliating the Jew and his belief makes self-idealization through the belief in God as a man more believable. This is especially true of people who have the greatest need to idealize themselves by identifying with a concrete version of God as a man and as one with a man's name just as they, too, have a name. These people at the same time tend to project what they consider evil in themselves and un-godlike to Jews so that they can gloriously identify themselves with a man, God, who is only good.

12 > EMBARRASSMENT AND ENVY

Anti-Semites often complain about Jewish compatriots who embarrass them. What is it that is embarrassing?

They complain about Jewish volubility, group visibility, lack of controlled feelings, pushiness, vulgarity—lack of manners, cowardice, etc.

These are surface phenomena. But they are not without meaning on a deeper level. What are these people really embarrassed about and is it possible that they actually envy the very characteristics they seemingly abhor in Jews? Is it possible that seeming loudness and seeming lack of controlled feelings are felt as the antithesis of alienation from feelings and of a sense of inner deadness? Do they envy freedom from censorship of expression? Do they envy the ability to engage in self-preservative moves of all kinds? Do they envy an ability to be articulate largely due to practicing uninhibited self-expression? Do they envy direct and unencumbered communication?

Is lack of manners actually the antithesis of a self-hating overlay of affectation? Is cowardice really evidence of self-preservation and yes—compassion? People suffering from severe symbol sickness are full of self-hate and compensatory self-idealization. Self-preservation seems cowardly to them. Jews through the ages have sacrificed themselves for principle and for other people. But heroic self-sacrifice for macho self-idealization is not ordinarily confused with courage in the Jewish mind.

In symbol sickness, death is often idealized and seen as a route to heaven. Part of Jewish survival is due to the reverence for life—all life. Again, it is not accidental that the universal Jewish toast is *le'Chaim*—to life! To the Jew the greatest courage is not related to death but rather to life. To live and to live an ethical, caring life is courageous. The Jews also feel courageous in their fight with God. Unlike anti-Semites, who secretly harbor rage at God—projected elsewhere as they passively accept all dogma—the Jew can fight with God. He/She carries on vigorous arguments and reassessments, and these result in constant reevaluations and beliefs regarding fundamentals of which all Jews are invited to be participants. These antithetical perceptions regarding courage, life, and death are used by the anti-Semite to fuel and to further rationalize projected self-hate and self-idealizing reactions to self-hate.

Jewish devotion to life brings further embarrassment. Nourishing life has other ramifications such as care for each other, for the young, for the helpless, for children, and for future generations. This makes for wife care, husband care, child care, a deep sense of *naches* and the ability to postpone gratification. I shall talk about *naches* in a later chapter.

The narcissistic symbol sufferer whose frustration tolerance is very poor is embarrassed by these missing virtues and converts them to signs of feminized, passive cowardice. Obviously, the symbol sufferer is not famous for his regard for women nor is he accepting of those aspects of self that he sees as feminine. These last confusions, we shall soon see, make violent acting out possible.

13 > JEW TALK

The anti-Semite is often both envious and suspicious of Jewish talking. His own inability and often unwillingness to make verbal connection to other people increases his feelings of isolation. It also hampers him because communication is vital in benefiting from the wisdom of other people. Talking becomes easier and increasingly effective with experience. Inexperience makes the process more difficult and as the victim becomes increasingly inarticulate, he feels bottled up, "paralyzed," nonproductive, and sometimes noncreative. Mutual affect response is missing from his life. This mutual affect response is perhaps one of the most envied and hated characteristics of Jews even though its psychodynamic often goes on unconsciously in the anti-Semite.

Talking is anti-autistic and anti-self-digestive, and is an exercise that establishes mutuality, intimacy—feelings of mutual support—bonding, regardless of what is said. In real talking—where feelings about self, each other, others and ideas, concepts and values are expressed—feelings are constantly generated. This generation of feelings born of mutual affect response—bouncing off each other—increases vitality and aliveness even as it opens up new vistas and ideas through verbal thought and feeling associations to each other's associations (words, ideas, etc.). This is what brainstorming and study groups are all about.

Paranoid, suspicious, constricted, detached, alienated people—people suffering from severe symbol sickness—cannot talk...really talk. Many Jews cannot talk, but this is not the perception of the anti-Semite. To him, all Jews are talkers; indeed, talking seems to him to be the leading Jewish activity. He envies their talk and the attachments and aliveness it brings and represents. But he is not conscious of what he envies. Indeed, often he is not conscious of being envious at all.

He covers up and obfuscates what he feels by investing pride in his own position of inhibition and verbal paralysis in denigrating Jewish talk.

He sees this talk as lack of control, as feminine weakness, as scheming and plotting, as degrading bargaining—as "Jewing down," as malicious gossip (if he is paranoid—about him and his), as not minding one's own business, but as being a noisy and nosy meddler, as being a talker rather then a doer and a worker, and on and on it goes.

Perhaps what is envied and despised most is the joy that Jews seem to have in talking and the connectedness it produces. The anti-Semite and all bigots are essentially joyless, life-denying, disconnected, autodigestive people.

Alienated, detached people, in order to dilute self-hate, attempt to idealize their difficulties. They make a virtue of inabilities and speak of dignified reserve, self-control, independence, and letting other people do their own thing. But given other factors, they attempt to reinforce their shaky beliefs by condemnation of the symbol that they choose to represent as the antithesis of their own idealized difficulties and limitations.

In extreme cases, Jews are not only seen as vulgar, obsessive talkers and loudmouths, but also, as paranoia is added, Jews are seen as plotters and schemers out to hurt and deprive the non-Jewish anti-Semite. It is again important to note here that the paranoid anti-Semite projects his self-hatred to the Jew and then believes the Jew hates him as much as he hates the Jew.

14 > THE EXISTENTIAL FORCE

The Jew ever in the mind of the anti-Semite is a continuous reminder of several very important abrasive forces. Together, these forces may be thought of as the existential force—the unmovable, the unchangeable, the unmitigating, the uncaring—the progenitors of and reminders of God, who, according to the anti-Semite, forgot and shortchanged him and perhaps people generally in so many ways. To the victim of the disease, the Jew goes on to mysteriously transcend mortality and human limits. "He is always there."

The following then is a short list of insults the anti-Semites feel that God has visited upon them but not upon Jews, who go on as a people endlessly exempt from items on this list.

- Mortality or finiteness and nonexistence after death regardless of any rationalizations. The deep symbol sufferer is incapable of true faith in a hereafter or anything else.

- The effects of conscience, which cannot be deadened completely by any known stratagem and the
self-hate, guilt, and anxiety therein produced.

- Luck or chance, which is haphazard, uncontrollable,
and seems to favor only chosen, special, lucky, unde-
serving people.

- Human limitations, including limited intelligence,
knowledge, talent, communication ability, self-control,
conflict, confusion, ambivalence, imperfections, un-
requited appetites, needs, and urges in all things in-
trinsically human.

- Uncontrollable catastrophes—so-called acts of
nature (hurricanes, earthquakes, floods, plagues,
malignancies)—and human disasters, political up-
heavals, religious rivalries, economic disasters, and
even stock market fluctuations.

On an unconscious level, Jews are seen by the anti-Semite as
the malevolent, uncontrollable force. The Jew is the perfect foil
for projection and displacement: personification of the Devil;
concretization of that aspect of God or the unfeeling universe;
detached from and oblivious to man, his limits and suffering.
On a conscious level, all this is translated into the belief that
the Jew is an unfeeling, ruthless, and oblivious exploiter and
opportunist, totally insensitive to the needs of others. This belief is present even as the Jew is also seen as the hapless, cowardly outcast and weakling. Reality of the Jewish tradition of
charity through the ages is completely ignored.

15 > THE DESIRE TO BE A JEW

The anti-Semite's most buried and unconscious secret—from himself and others—is the desire to be a Jew. He wants to be free of conscience and inner coercions, and he believes that Jews are free. He, too, wants to be what he views as the exotic and peculiarly privileged outsider. He wants to be the total and forever expatriate even as he raves about his own patriotism and nationalistic feelings and influences.

It is, I believe, those very feelings and influences that he wishes to nullify and escape. Deep down he despises his own identity and everything that contributes to that identity—national, religious, racial. All of it has for him become part and parcel of all the inner constrictions that restrain and stifle him. He blames everything that identifies him even as he idealizes everything that identifies him as a robber of his individuality, creativity, and freedom. He sees it all as coercive and as a producer of self-hate and punishment.

He believes that to be a Jew is to able to transcend everything material, religious, and racial; to be a Jew is to be free; to be a Jew is to be the ultimate individual; to be a Jew is to be removed from group identification dilution. He craves this select Jewish connection/disconnection (from the larger group) even as he is terrified of it.

This Jewish connection means freedom but it also means self-reliance, risk, anxiety born of lack of dependency-satisfying structure. Freedom means the potential unleashing of uncontrollable appetites and forces.

The conflict between dependency and independence threatens to tear him apart.

In despising the Jew, he obliterates all aspects of his "Jewish desires" for independence, individuality, and freedom, and he feels safe.

In intense anti-Semitism of a seriously obsessive nature, the secret (unconscious) desire to be a Jew, to have everything the Jew has (including all that is envied: martyrdom, independence, God-connection, opportunistic self-interest, freedom from moral dictates, etc.) may be overwhelming. Here, identity with the hated object may be almost complete. When this occurs, the desire may turn into the fear and even the delusion of becoming or of being the hated object—a Jew. This may have been the case with Adolf Eichmann and others like him and I shall describe my theoretical view of Eichmann's case a little later on.

In some cases the victim may feel possessed, taken over, changed into the hated object, the entire process then expanding his already considerable self-hate. To rid the self of fear of turning Jewish (and the temptation to have all that he secretly envies is enormous) and to dilute his self-hate, to exorcise the Jew, and to cleanse the self of all Jewishness, he must obliterate the hated object.

In some cases, the temptation to become the hated object is so intense that it may produce panic. This temptation is also fed by a desire to relieve both self-corrosive envy and self-consuming hatred.

I believe that if any health exists in a person—despite his sickness—the kernel of health will produce at least some desire to nullify hatred of both himself and others. Hatred is not the normal human condition. Unfortunately, the stratagems used to seek inner equilibrium are often themselves convoluted and highly destructive.

16 > SURVIVAL AS A PEOPLE

Survival of the Jews as an identifiable people produces envy of seeming immortality but to the Jew hater is has other significance as well.

Survival despite all-out efforts at extermination provides possibilities, proofs, and frustrations for the anti-Semite that fuel fear, anxiety, rage, and hatred. Relative to the degree of sickness, the following is a list of at least partially unconscious feelings and beliefs.

- The Jew is "special after all." His specialty is summed up by his presence generation after generation as the external and insidious stranger. Survival is interpreted as special.

- Resistance to obliteration is felt as inappropriate obstinacy. While death would indicate appropriate compliance to not being wanted, assimilation would at least be felt as conventional but perhaps polluting to the general population.

- Survival is felt as an arrogant insult—a splinter in the eye, an individualistic non-fitting and creating of an imperfection to potential total integration and smooth wholeness of the entire population.

- Survival in a world in which nothing survives is proof of God's protection—or is it evidence of protection of the Devil and an extension of him and all that is different and therefore evil?

- Dependency on Jews as scapegoats—as the means to express and to justify irrational anger—makes their survival desirable, creating internal conflict in the anti-Semite. He feels confused and ambivalent. He needs the Jew as victim and needs him to die, to become extinct, too. Remember, for many anti-Semites, the Jew provides a central, common, integrating focus—a raison d'etre.

These feelings are not verbalized internally or to others. They are simply there. The continued existence of the Jew is felt an as an aberration, as an insult, as a frustration, and as a threat. Unconsciousness itself serves as an antilogic device. As with the dreams it creates, the unconscious is full of repressed material over which no central force exerts a rational influence. Thus, confusion abounds. Jew, the enemy, exists, and his existence is an insult but the insult is desired so as to give rationale for many unknown sources of anger and an outlet for it.

17 > PEOPLE OF THE DIALECTICAL CONTINUUM

Anti-Jews feel like fragmented people of the moment. They feel disconnected, isolated, alone, and frightened. They feel there are only antagonists around them and that potential help from any source is nonexistent. They feel like autodigestive, self-destruct devices. Being disconnected, they do their thing and then it is over for them. This sense of aloneness is fed and then in turn feeds exaggerated narcissism, attenuating furthers a sense of connection.

Sufferers from symbol sickness, in their "me against the world" feelings, tend to concentrate on hierarchical standing and to be highly competitive, adversarial, and antagonistic. This makes for a high degree of suspiciousness, distrust, and often paranoia. "Trust no one! Everybody is out to get you! Everyone is for number one!" This makes for much projection and the belief that other people, especially Jews, feel, and operate the same way they do.

This attitude and resulting behavior destroys the rewards possible and forthcoming only from a high degree of cooperation, mutual assistance, joint commitment, and effort. Coupled with an inability to *postpone gratification* (a highly prized Jewish virtue that I will soon discuss), ambitious goals cannot be realized. The postponement of gratification, required in long-range projects, development of self, and complex plans, is impossible for people who feel disconnected from the past and future and from other people—who might otherwise strengthen a sense of identification and optimism. These people must live in the moment because they feel that the moment is all they have.

Connectedness to other people and to a people's history lengthens the feel of the present that is felt as one's people's and one's own self-continuum. This provides optimism in dealing with goals requiring long-range plans and efforts and mutual cooperation. This makes enormous rewards possible.

Jews are the personification of the long-range view. They excel at cooperation and at being part of the whole. They had to cooperate in order to survive. They connect the past, present, and future and connect to each other. They profit from the wisdom and experience of forefathers and the group. This makes Nobel Prize cooperative efforts possible. This also makes them the envy—often the malignant envy—of the self-disenfranchised (from self, others, and past and future) anti-Semite to whom they become prime objects of projected self-hate. The Jew is an intense cooperator. The anti-Semite's philosophy confuses commitment, dedication, intense interest, involvement, and optimism with sick competition. Sick competition is the only gut practical experience the anti-Semite has had relative to other people and efforts.

I believe that anti-Semites are people of the encapsulated moment. Jews are people of the dialectical continuum. This makes for intense misunderstanding and sometimes murderous hatred.

The dialectical continuum is highly influenced by the Talmud—the ever-present running, dialectical, ethical, moral, eternal discourse of the Jews. This document, its arguments and values, augmented by tradition, language, humor, and all else we call culture, exerts influence from generation to generation on Talmudists and non-Talmudists alike. Its being there constantly augmented has made the Jews connect the past, present, future, and to the whole (group) on a deep, psychological level. This tradition of psychological connection has for centuries developed a life of its own no longer even requiring the Talmud itself for continued existence. This connectedness makes for powerful family ties, group ties, long-range plans, and the rewards of intense cooperation and postponement of gratification when necessary. It also makes for sick envy.

18 > CONTINUUM, *NACHES*, POSTPONEMENT OF GRATIFICATION

The insistence on the importance of life and self-idealization through consistent values and ethics has made for a long history of survival as Jews. As I pointed out earlier, the Talmud is probably the longest-running ethical and value-oriented discourse in the history of our species. This insistence on living despite horrendous vicissitudes, this unparalleled tenacity and self-identification and self-examination create frustration and envy in those who hate Jews.

Symbol sickness precludes postponement of gratification. Symbol sickness produces poor frustration tolerance and requires instant results and satisfaction. This makes larger satisfactions requiring training, study, work, struggle, and development impossible. Viewing life in fragments of time makes it virtually impossible to develop a sense of continuum so necessary for postponement of gratification. This ability is further aberrated by narcissism, which precludes identification with the group and satisfaction through the achievement of members of one's group. The concept of sacrifice of the present and of oneself in order for progeny to reap rewards in the future is foreign to people having no sense of real connection, continuum, and who suffer a pronounced inability to postpone gratification.

Waiting for the messiah (who never arrives) is a lesson in the process of postponement of gratification. It is also a lesson in hope. This is reinforced by a sense of continuum.

The Jewish continuum and 5,000-year-old group identification is ideal for postponement of gratification. It makes for an optimism of continuing existence and great frustration tolerance giving one the ability to try again and again and again.

The Jew feels himself as an unhurried presence in terms of time necessary for fruition and satisfaction in group accomplishments. Investment in the past makes investment in the future possible. Group identification and satisfaction through identification with the group is anti-narcissistic and makes investment in others possible.

This also leads to a uniquely Jewish phenomenon known as *naches*. *Shepping naches* largely means reaping satisfaction through the self-realization of people other than oneself. *Naches* becomes heightened if the other person is a group member. *Naches* through children is the most satisfying of all. Freud said that his success was largely due to his mother's belief in him, a self-fulfilling prophecy. This is not remarkable for Jews, who as I said earlier have been waiting and continue to wait for the messiah. *Naches* may make for overindulgence of children but also for a successful possibility in terms of parental-fulfilling prophecies. This, of course, is coupled with enormous parental support and reinforces Buddha who put great value on the ability to wait.

Thus, Jews are capable of postponing gratification over generations, decades, and even centuries. This in turn makes for heightened group identification, feelings of continuum, dedication to long life, and long-standing commitments necessary for complex achievements. I believe that this largely accounts for a history of significant Jewish influence in areas requiring much struggle and study.

To the anti-Semite, Jewish achievements are not seen in this light at all. They are seen as the result of slimy manipulation and cabal-like insider cooperation, designed to frustrate non-Jews. To the anti-Semite, Jews seem to live forever and to have undue influence and to steal all the goodies for themselves. Envy is enormous and insight regarding the power of continuums, time, postponing gratification, and the anti-narcissistic effects of *naches* and group identification is often entirely lacking.

The tradition of respect for the "wise man" or for rabbinical wisdom or for the great savant is an important addendum and reinforcement of the postponement of gratification factor. It provides the possibility of building on other people's knowledge and experience so that enormous time is saved not having to recapitulate mistakes already made. It also obviously makes for rapid building blocks and easier addition of new knowledge. But this can only happen if there is sufficient trust for others, again usually born of traditional group identification. This cannot occur where there is sever symbol sickness, a high degree of narcissism, distrust, detachment, and a feeling of separateness and of being encapsulated and cut off from others.

In conclusion here let me say that the entire feeling about time and place could not be more different for the Jew and the anti-Jew. Place for the Jew in long-range terms is mainly connected to people identification rather than as a geographical entity. The group is felt as existing from an ancient past into a distant future. This makes for particular applications of self and adaptations of self to goals and to places of various cultures. The Jew can feel at home anywhere because he is at home in long-range time. And he is at home in his feeling of one and with his people, who have been there and will be there throughout time. While Israel and Jerusalem are definite geographic places of great importance and always have been, their greater significance is symbolic. Regardless of where Jews live, Jerusalem represents the Jewish people and through that place they identify with Jews everywhere even though they may feel more at home in New York.

The anti-Semite sees this geographical spread as unpatriotic because he is rooted to place geographically, having neither roots in himself, other people, or in time—past or future. His time, unlike the Jewish long now, is the time of the immediate, the very short, fragmentary now. This deprives him of long-range views, endeavors, accomplishments (especially those requiring group cooperation), and satisfactions therein derived. It leaves him feeling empty, confused, cut off, frustrated, paranoid, severely envious, and too often enraged.

19 > "RACE OF DIALECTICAL LIARS"
—ADOLF HITLER

H itler made the above statement about Jews in his *Mein Kampf*, but this is not an unusual opinion among anti-Semites.

Let us make a brief further comment here on the Talmud. Jews have produced probably the longest-running dialectical argument in history. The Talmud addresses itself to ethical and moral issues and rarely sees them in black-and-white terms. Mitigating circumstances, human limitations, ambivalent feelings, uncontrollable outside forces, existential dynamics, and even the unconscious are applied as major considerations while countless deliberations take place.

The evolving values, morals, ethics, and laws have had a profound effect on Western philosophy, values, psychology, and Anglo-Saxon law. My father, a great student of the Talmud, believed that much of Freudian psychology is derivative of the Talmud. The Jungian notion of racial unconscious may be explained by the existence of this document in terms of a trans generational process. The passing on of highly influential concepts and ethical forces through the written word does not require Jungian mysterious and mystical forces to explain a racial commonality of unconscious and conscious values, ideas, and feelings.

Jews are thus influenced to appreciate that much of life and its issues are neither black nor white. There is more gray in life than extremes of multitudinous polarizations. This kind of "Talmudic" approach and examination also lends to careful examination of details, to the settling of differences peacefully through cooperative application to problems, and to appreciation for complexity and subtlety. These are sometimes viewed as nit-picking processes, but they are attempts at dealing with the human condition in the most humane ways with high priority on practical reality.

There is a high price to pay for this kind of perception and reasoning. This price includes a high possibility of internal conflict, mind or decision changing, generation of pressures of conscience, and high proclivity for anxiety and frustration. To the anti-Semite, this is particularly strange, coming from the peple he feels are conscience producers. From his black-and-white approach to living, he sees the Jew again escaping conscience and vacillating through a convenient moral screen to manipulate for his own selfish gains.

In any case, the price that must be paid—sometimes confusion until clarity presents itself in order to see things in realistic gray terms—is not one the symbol sickness sufferer cares to make. This approach—let us call it the gray approach—flies in the face of the deadening of feelings and the attraction of shallow living and the easy black-and-white solution to problems. These are terrifying to people who have an inability to wait and who cannot stand frustration or anxiety.

The Jew and his kind of application of logic is seen by the anti-Semite as a great confuser, teaser, frustrator, delayer, and manipulator for his own purposes.

Profundity and the application of human realities to human problems, which are always complex, is the last thing the anti-Semite or incipient anti-Semite wants. Gray involves constantly shifting and processing mitigating circumstances. This involves compassion—and the anti-Semite views compassion as feminized, passive weakness.

To view people who seek a level of understanding more profound than surface phenomena as "liars" is a convenient rationalization of one's own self-imposed ignorance. Bringing considerations to issues that make for a struggle and inner turmoil is felt as an attack. Complexity is seen as poison. Investigation is felt as boring frustration. Reason is felt as obfuscation. All of it is lumped together and seen as a method of wily scheming and lying manipulation. This view is a form of resistance used to defend against anxiety born of the struggle to change and potential for real and healthy insight and growth.

The Talmud, through its influence on Jewish culture, has had a profound influence on most Jews—even those who barely know of its existence. Thus, the Jews tend to be people who find it difficult and even impossible to accept dogma. They learn to know that people are fallible and things are not always what they seem and that truths may with examination turn out not to be truths at all. To the compliant, conforming Jew hater, this antidogma attitude is seen as evidence of faithlessness, disloyalty, troublemaking, and destructive rebelliousness. This belief convince the anti-Semite of his own self-righteousness and strengthens his view of himself as pure and loyal rather than shallow and compulsively compliant. Discussion, research, doubting, and clarifying are all seen as intellectual claptrap, egg headedness, joy killing, stubbornness, and even infidelity (the inability to accept other men's dogma blindly).

Sharpening intellect through discourse and use of mind is seen as scheming, and their old fear of the so-called Jewish mind is exacerbated among anti-Semites.

In conclusion, it is interesting to note that Hitler was the self-admitted inventor and user of the big lie. His biggest lies were about Jews. In lying, he catered to the needs of anti-Semites. He manipulated them as he satisfied the monstrous appetites of his grotesque and hideous psychosis.

20 > KILLING THEM AGAIN AND AGAIN

I believe that repeated persecution and killing of Jews has a separate, autonomous, dynamic motive aside from the dynamics already described that feed hatred.

The periodicity of flare-ups of anti-Semitism leading to pogroms and worse could conceivably have an unconscious dynamic and what we may call a "special rationale." What could these symbolic, almost ritualistic murders be about?

Let me suggest a dual rationale.

- Each wave of destructive outbursts against Jews is a rebellion against inner coercions born of a repressive conscience. In effect, it is displaced rebellion against inner tyranny. Repressive effects of inner tyranny become exacerbated when theocracy of any kind demands unusual moral submission. It also becomes exacerbated when nationalistic forces demand a patriotism whose ideas are tyrannical and repressive. The Jew, at these times, through connection to

Christ, is once again felt as the source of conscience and repression, making obliteration appropriate and extremely inviting.

- Jesus as martyr has enormous appeal. Indeed, sanctification is mainly based on martyrdom. Martrydom is seen as the ultimate self-sacrifice for the well-being of the group—the height of glory and self-idealization. Martrydom is interpreted as proof of love, fidelity, and dedication. It justifies one's own hardships, constrictions, and emulated self-sacrifce. Keeping martyrdom of the leader alive in the forefront of awareness is all-important. It has a unifying, binding effect and sustains the power and glory of the group leaders. Carried to the ultimate, in some cultures the king is killed, martyred, and thus each king accumulates the glory and respect of his predecessor.

Is it possible that sacrificing Jews sustains the martyrdom of Jesus in several ways?

- It produces martyrdom of a sacrificial victim in order to remind and reinforce memory of martyrdom of the ultimate leader.

- The victim is a special victim, who in being martyred is being executed for supposedly having martryred the leader, in being related to the leader—being his progenitor—being martyred represents the martyring and remartyring of Jesus again and again. This ritualistic displacement has high symbolic value and gives the victimizer confident security in his beliefs rather than guilt or regret.

The sustaining of His martyrdom, of His sacrifice is an enormously important power in the name of the cross—the crucifixion as symbol by the high offices of the group. People will kill for those who suffer even more than for those who conquer. For the deluded violent anti-Semite, devoid of real Christian values or feelings, Jews provide an endless reservoir of victims to support shaky beliefs used as rationale for symbol sickness and self-idealization.

21 > ADVERSARY RELATING AND COOPERATIVE RELATING

Jews could seldom afford to be purely individualistic or narcissistic or completely self-serving. Chronic persecution and a resulting siege mentality made this impossible if one wished merely to survive, to live. Outside discrimination pressures virtually guaranteed group identification, group cohesiveness, group cooperation, and a consequent very powerful subcultural value system. Of prime value to such a group is any contribution to the survival of members of the group.

The Jewish toast le'Chaim—to life—is basic to Jewish psychology and is also a reaction to the anti-Semite's toast to death—for the Jews. "To life" becomes meaningless unless the group cooperates to live. This makes for a particular value system, frame of reference, and group of pride investments or self-idealizing goals that are somewhat different than other populations and easily misunderstood. This cooperative drive may be hidden by superficial intragroup squabbles, competition, and seeming divisiveness. But these are only ventilating, shallow exercises of intellectual muscle flexing. Underlying co-operation is the main theme and in a way Judaism has always been a kind of spread-out kibbutz on a deep emotional level. Nowhere is this evidenced more than in family life, despite exceptions we can all point to here and there.

This means that to Jews self-esteem is seen in terms of what brings honor to the family and as families to the group. Intellectual achievement, high standard of living, artistic ability, creativity, being charitable, contribution to health and longevity—these are all ventures requiring cooperation and leading to contribution to self-realization of people other than solely oneself. This is especially important in terms of young people. Investment in the young is crucial to people who have long memories of an ancient existence and an outlook for a much longer future.

Arguments among Jews are common. These are extensions of dialectical attempts at mutual understanding. Physical fights are rare because mutual damage is antithetical to group cooperation, survival, and well-being. This inhibition to maim each other physically is erroneously interpreted as cowardice. Actually, it is reverence for life and limb and sustained existence of the group. But there are other more important misunderstandings that fuel the anti-Semite's rationalizations.

The isolated anti-Semite functions largely on a self-serving, narcissistic level. He feels alienated from any group. His pride investments are competitive and devoted to being "better" or "ahead" of the others. He feels by putting others down his hierarchical striving justifies damage, physical and otherwise, to others under the guise of self-idealizing independence. His greatest connection to the group actually comes through adversary and antagonistic relating. Tradition and family mean little to him unless they can be incorporated into a self-glorifying, narcissistic schema. Thus, he too easily sees Jews as cowardly, effeminate, and conspirational. The value systems of the two groups clash on almost every level.

22 > GENDER CONFUSION, HOMOPHOBIA, AND MADNESS

How can we account though for the periodic outbursts of violence, torture, and murder? Even among the sufferers of the most virulent anti-Semitism, what possibly mobilizes their hatred so as to push them past all inhibitions, making a willingness to participate in pogroms and worse? How can seemingly ordinary, passive anti-Semites be turned into organized, Holocaust-sadistic murderers?

Explanations about their inner deadness and need for sadistic stimulation cannot account for their violent acting out! Seeing and feeling the Jew as the hated symbol of freedom and of the oppressive conscience visited upon them cannot account for the murderous explosions. Envy of the Jews for innumerable distorted delusions of privilege still is not enough.

Depersonalization and dehumanization of the Jew sets the stage. It is easier to kill a hated nonperson. It is made still easier if one has killed off one's own feelings of empathy and sympathy, leaving only rage. But this, too, does not account for the murderous explosion necessary for the annihilation process to take place.

I believe the answer lies in fear—in fact, terrible fear, actually the worst kind of terror. This kind of violence is a striking out against one's own projected terror of disgrace and annihilation.

I speak here of inner terror of infinitely greater magnitude than the fear of an avenging God—possibly the Jewish God. I speak here of fear much greater than burning in the hell of Dante's Inferno for ever and ever. After all, these fears are only fears of the imagination.

I believe that the fear that motivates murder and even genocide springs from unconscious forces of terror, which every clinician has seen who has worked in hospitals for psychotic people who are acting-out their terror hostility.

I speak here of homosexual panic leading to severe paranoid states.

In this condition, the victim is in terror of homosexual feelings and homosexual attraction. He must repress his own knowledge of these urges at all costs. When they threaten to emerge, he must do anything and everything at all possible to repress and to relegate these feelings back into unconsciousness. This in large part accounts for severe homophobia and acting out violent criminal assaults and murders of homosexuals. But, some of the most brutal rages and paranoid attacks take place against people who are not at all homosexual. They simply have had the misfortune to be attractive to the terrified repressed person in panic of self-exposure.

This is the mechanism in simplest form: The individual in desperate confusion of his gender identification, living in a world that exaggeratedly polarizes masculine and feminine characteristics, attempts to repress all feelings and characteristics viewed as feminine. He idealizes "masculinity." He incorporates "macho" characteristics into his own self-idealization and self-indentifying structure and attempts to exclude any diluting forces.

Macho includes strength, mastery, toughness, old-boy camaraderie, sexual bravado, etc. He may even live in a fatherland rather than a motherland and intense nationalism and militarism may also help in his attempt to polarize. *But* this is not enough. Let us suppose that, due to failure of some kind—economic failure, professional failure, or any failure in his life—his pride in self-reliance and mastery starts to crumble. Let us suppose his image of himself begins to give way sufficiently so that the "feminine side" of himself starts to emerge. These may include passivity, feelings of dependency, the need for love and warmth, a sense of helplessness, etc. At this point, feelings for or about members of his own sex or fear of such feelings—felt as homosexual feelings—may emerge. These threaten his very identity both in terms of self-idealization and gender identification, which is already confused. There are few of us who do not suffer from at least some gender confusion.

In a society or subculture where pride investment in polarized gender identification is extreme, there is no greater fear than self-recognition of homosexuality on any level—real or imagined. This recognition engenders self-revulsion and self-hate of extraordinary magnitude. How to guard against it? The last resort is projecting the fear to persons outside oneself whom one sees as homosexuals who wish to seduce, rape, and attack the individual who is breaking down. Now, the person threatened by his own feelings believes it is the other individual (often anyone he may be attracted to or anyone he can designate as homosexual) who has designs on him. His self-fear has now become paranoid terror of the other individual whom he may attack before he himself is attacked, thus saving himself from self-revelation and self-revulsion engendered by what he feels would leave him a castrated, degenerate nonentity. I have seen men cower in corners in homosexual panic and attack with unbelievable terror, rage, and ferocity anyone at all who even entered the room, let alone unwittingly touched them.

How does this connect to killing Jews? The Jew becomes the detested symbol to whom homophobia is projected as an attempt to prevent sever self-hate and homosexual panic. Indeed, I believe that in a great many cases killing Jews is evidence of severe gender confusion, homophobia, and is a form of acting out homosexual panic.

Is it possible that to the potentially violent anti-Semite, the Jew, his blood relative Jesus (and unconsciously Jesus is felt as a Jew), and the Christian church represent passivity, femininity, and confused gender identification? Christ, the Prince of Peace, is seen as a feminized God. Peace is felt as passivity and as antithetical to male dreams of glory through aggression. Occasional aggressive forays in the name of Christ and his peace—crusades, inquisitions, witch-hunts—do not suffice to integrate.

23 > ECONOMIC DEPRIVATION, NATIONALISM, AND ALIENS

The disease flares up and tends to advance to a more progressive stage and becomes metastatic during periods of nationalistic fervor (regardless of causes), economic deprivation, national disasters, conquests, and crisis periods.

These are periods of stress, and stress, frustration, deprivation, reminders of human limitations, and mortality, are aspects of reality that immature symbol sickness sufferers find intolerable. During these periods there is an enormous increase in self-hate, depression, abused reactions, projection, paranoia, and envy of those who are rightly or wrongly believed to have more or to be at all privileged. These kinds of times produce much projection and displacement in people who are strongly self-hating and find their self-hate intolerable. This is in fact their principal way of seeking relief.

Of course, there are many roots and functions for nationalism. But a very powerful psychodynamic source that it promotes is the belief in being special. Being special results

119

in compensatory self-puffery and is used to combat poor self-esteem. Poor self-esteem on a national basis requires self-inflation on a national basis. Comparisons to nationals of other countries often fail to produce special superiority. This is especially so if other nationals are in fact in better economic and political circumstances.

But minority nationals of one's own country who are marked as second-class or even nonrated citizens usually serve the purpose well. This is so because they usually suffer from at least the same vicissitudes as the majority of the nationals or are even more deprived than the first-class citizens.

The Jews serve this purpose of comparison superbly well for a number of reasons.

There is the ingrained habit of turning on Jews and using them for displacement and projection as scapegoats. Habit is very important, especially to neurotics and psychotics. Anti-Semites fall into both categories. In severe alienation, spontaneity and free choice are largely lacking. Behavior takes place on a more primitive conditioned reflex basis. The fact that it has been done before or, better yet, if it is an ongoing process, makes continuation or a restart easy.

Symbol sickness produces compliant, conforming, highly suggestible people. If Jew hating is common in a society, people of that society will be highly vulnerable to the contagious effect. If society condones the disease passively or actively, consciously or unconsciously, the conformist will seize and run with it and will surely bite and infect many of his compatriots.

Since Jews, regardless of religious belief and national identification, retain common cultural practices and values, it is usually easy to identify them as a separate group. Recognition is made easier by Jews tending to marry Jews who also share a long memory of common history and ethnic customs.

The fact that Jews embrace the national identification of their country of residence with utmost loyalty means nothing to the anti-Semites. That the Jew can be *the other,* separated from the mainstream, isolated and alienated—seen as alien—means everything. To him (the conformist) to be different is to be bad. This is axiomatic! To be different here helps to serve hierarchical striving that becomes exaggerated during attacks of inadequacy. Jew, as outsider, is easy to relegate to a position of inferiority and provides the possibility of feeling relatively superior.

Since rationale of any kind is meaningless to the anti-Semite, economic deprivation as well as other difficulties are blamed on Jews. This aids the process of separation and isolation completing a vicious cycle.

Using Jews as alien people and outsiders provides the anti-Semite a synthetic source of belonging and being an insider with attachment to the main group. This reinforcement of identification with the national majority becomes necessary during attacks of inadequacy and eruptions of dependency feelings. Being an "insider" gives synthetic strength that is fed by isolating the Jew in the crowd, separating him from the crowd and viewing him as "outside."

The long-standing and habitual process of depersonalizing and dehumanizing Jews (part of the process of separating them from the whole and sustaining their alienation) makes it easier to deaden what shades of conscience and moral equivocation might still exist in the anti-Semite.

24 > HITLER'S DISEASE

The combination of psychosis, psychopathy, and genius, consisting of psychological and persuasive glibness, is luckily relatively rare.

Fortunately, most-anti-Semites are neurotic rather than psychotic or sociopathic (psychopathic). They have no particular genius for malevolence, mob psychology, or special manipulative abilities. The depth of their symbol sickness is relatively moderate. Dehumanization in them is ordinarily far from total; conscience and moral equivocation, while aberrated, exist; empathy, sympathy, and compassion—while not intact—are at least vestigial. These moderately sick people are capable of moral judgment based on at least a minimum of residual reality testing. But even these neurotic anti-Semites, given good germinating ground and proper circumstances, will abandon what health they have to follow a malignantly sick leader. In so doing many will become psychotic automatons themselves—temporarily or permanently losing the ability to turn back. Much depends on their synchronicity and their vulnerability.

Unfortunately, a monstrous combination of psychodynamic vectors sometimes takes place. It is particularly destructive when it appears in a person who lives in a place of great germinating possibility. It is most malignant if that person's delusional system incorporates severe hatred of a particular group of people and readily converts to his hatred, values, and schemes.

Hitler, most authorities agree, considered Marxism a Jewish invention and weapon. His two favorite subjects in his psychotic masterwork *Mein Kampf* are Marxism and the Jews. Of course, he was well aware that Karl Marx was a Jew and this fact surely lent credence to Hitler's paranoid, psychotic system. This also lent credence to the belief that Hitler's war (World War II) was primarily a war against the Jews. This was brilliantly argued by Lucy Davidovitz in her book *The War Against the Jews*.

Now let me quote from *Mein Kampf* (quoted from *The Making of the Atomic Bomb*, pp. 175–176, by Richard Rhodes).

> Jews are "no lovers of water." [Hitler] "often grew sick to my stomach from [their] smell." Their dress is "unclean," their appearance "generally unheroic." "A foreign people," they have "definite racial characteristics;" they are "inferior being(s)," "vampires," "with poisonous fangs," "yellow fist(s)," and "repulsive traits." "The personification of the Devil as the symbol of all evil assumes the living shape as the Jew."
>
> The Jew is a "garbage separator, splashing his filth on the face of humanity." He is "a scribbler—who poisons men's souls like germ-carriers of the worst sort"—"the cold-hearted, shameless, and calculating director of this revolting vice traffic in the scum of the big city." "Was there any form of filth or profligacy, without at least one

Jew involved in it? If you cut even cautiously into such an abscess, you found, like a maggot in a rotting body, often dazzled by the sudden light—a kike!"

The Jew was "no German." Jews are "a race of dialectical liars," a "people which lives only for this earth," the "great masters of the lie," "traders, profiteers, usurers, and swindlers," "a world hydra," "a horde of rats," "alone in this world they would stifle in filth and offal."

"Without any true culture" the Jew is "a parasite in the body of other peoples," "a sponger like a noxious bacillus keeps spreading as soon as a favorite medium invites him." "He lacks idealism in any form." "He is an eternal blood-sucker" of "diabolic purposes," restrained by no moral scruples," who "poisons the blood of others but preserves his own." He "systematically ruins women and girls." "With satanic joy on his face, the black-haired Jewish youth lurks in wait for the unsuspecting girl whom he defiles with his blood, thus stealing her from her people." He is a "master of the bastards and bastards alone," and "It was and is Jews who bring the Negroes into the Rhineland, always with the same secret thought and clear aim of ruining the hated white race by the necessarily resulting bastardization." Syphilis is a "Jewish disease," a "Jewification of our spiritual life and mammonization of our mating instinct [that] will sooner or later destroy our entire offspring." The Jew "makes a mockery of natural feelings, overthrows all concepts of beauty and sublimity of the noble and the good, and instead drags men down into the sphere of his own base nature." "An apparition in a black caftan and black hair-locks," responsible for "spiritual pustulence worse than the black death of olden times," the Jew is a "coward," "a plunderer," "a menace," "a foreign element," "a viper," "a tyrant," "a fermented decomposition."

Hitler wrote a poem out of a dream he had during World War I:

I often go on bitter nights
To Wotan's oak in the quiet glad
With dark powers to weave a union
The runic letters the moon makes with its magic spell
And all that are full of impudence during the day
Are made small by the magic formula!

He dictated the following:

If at the beginning of the war and during the war 12 or 15,000 of these Hebrew corrupters of the people had been held under poison gas, as happened to hundreds of thousands of our very best German workers in the field, the sacrifice of millions at the front would not have been in vain.

Hitler's megalomania fed by a psychotic process made for godlike delusions of grandeur. His sociopathy destroyed any empathic or identifying ability as well as any potential for conscience or moral equivocation. The combination of both produced an extraordinary narcissism and dehumanization. He was not human—he was a god. People were not human or individuals with their own autonomy at all. They were to him extensions of himself—good and bad extensions depending on what aspects of himself he invested in them.

Reality had no meaning to him. The only reality that existed was his reality, the one he invented and dreamed up as he went along—one made up of Wagnerian, primitive Wotan primeval mystical operatic forces and florid hallucinatory, delusional, self-inflating lies and distortions. As with many psychotics, Hitler soon believed his own machinations, monstrous productions, and lies, including those he borrowed from the almost equally sick anti-Semitic Wagner and the invented *Protocols of the Elders of Zion.*

Once he believed in the monsters he created—as with near-ly all paranoids—he was in terror of them and hated them for this terror—all of his own making. To the extent of his hid-eous projected needs, his beliefs, and his terror, he had to ratio-nalize these beliefs and invent still more lies to retain a belief in his nonexistent sanity.

He was a master psychologist of mass behavioral phenom-ena, of propaganda, of inflammatory oratory, and most im-portant, of understanding the anti-Semitic needs of others like him. The combination of deadened conscience characteristic of sociopathy, dehumanization of self and others, and mega-lomania found in psychosis and specialized brilliance as mob manipulator made him deadly. But, of course, there were and are many others without that brilliance who nevertheless share much of his disease. He was and is not alone.

Hitler used the Jews for more than political purposes, that is, to integrate the German people around a central theme of a hated enemy. He used the Jews as a synthetic focal point for his own meaningless, dehumanized life—a life empty of mean-ingful relationships, of no self-esteem, and of compensating delusions of grandeur.

Is it possible that in his quest to compensate for inner dead-ness he had to be the ultimate sadist, the death dealer, who had to murder whole multitudes and to eradicate an entire national-ity? Is it possible that to compensate for inner collapse and pro-found feelings of self-defilement (projected to Jews) he needed to be satanically (ascribed to Jews) omnipotent—greater than God—a new and dehumanized death-dealing devil-god? If so, then Jews became the logical enemies to this devious, dehuman-ized mind. These believers in the messiah, these producers of Jesus must be wiped out so as to remove all roots and possibility of another false god even as they satisfied the dynamic needs of all common sufferers of anti-Semitic symbol sickness.

Killing Jews makes way for the devil-god, the dehumanized god, the noncompassionate self-glorifying narcissistic god, the nationalized god, the great hierarchical (*Deutschland über alles*) Aryan god, the Wagnerian primeval German-god—Hitler himself. Thus, he wipes out the stain of the failed painter, the street bum, the unrecognized, persecuted genius. Thus, he is finally vindicated and lives out all his childhood fantasies of omnipotent triumph over psychotically fabricated enemies whom he omnipotently kills through manipulations of His chosen people—the good, clean, German working people whom he secretly feels estranged from because he really believes that he himself is filth and slime. These German people were felt by Hitler as extensions of his own utterly narcissistic persona and they became instruments of death as Hitler in his perversion of reality attempted to scourge himself of what he felt as human filth through projection to Jews.

He speaks of defilement, purity, German women, etc., and I suspect there was much in the way of sexual feelings that terrified him. Didn't he seek relief through the assassination of the largely homosexual SA storm troopers, albeit there was political motivation there, too? Is it possible that with every Jew he killed he repeatedly killed off his own sexual feelings? Is it possible that he killed Jesus again and again? In any case, he is the embodiment of all the dynamics of the disturbance, albeit the most exaggerated form, fed by and extended through his genius in terms of manipulating almost an entire population. Yes, he was the rare combination of psychosis, sociopathy, and special evil genius.

The Protocols of the Elders of Zion, an anti-Semitic document manufactured in Russia to justify pogroms (derived from a French work, *Dialogues from Hell between Montesquieu and*

Macchiavelli, published in 1864 and written by Maurice Joli) became Hitler's bible. Hannah Ardendt wrote:

> Thus, the *Protocols* presented world conquest as a practical possibility, implied that the whole affair was only a question of inspired or shrewd know-how, and that nobody stood in the way of a German victory over the entire world but a potentially small people, the Jews, who ruled it without possessing instruments of violence—an easy opponent, therefore, once their secret was discovered and their method emulated on a larger scale.

As Richard Rhodes says in his superb work, *The Making of the Atomic Bomb*:

> But the scurrilities of *Mein Kampf*, which on the evidence of their incoherence are not calculated manipulations but violent emotional outbursts, demonstrate that Hitler pathologically feared and hated the Jews. In black megalomania he masked an intelligent, industrious and much persecuted people with the distorted features of his own terror. And that would make all the difference.

I believe his megalomania went further than that and even further than his ambition for a "1,000-year Reich." His megalomania, fed by his psychosis, produced visions of being lord of the galaxy—a Wagnerian, Wotan God whose angels would be blond-haired German purebloods, the antithesis of the "dark-haired Jew" and the Jewish Christ, Christian God. Yes, he surely hated Christianity, too, but in his craftiness, characteristic of paranoia, he chose to persecute Catholics only when he could. He could not do so on a mass scale—too many of his Germans, Austrians, and allied Italians were Catholic. Nearly all of his nation was Christian—Protestant—and he could not turn on his much-needed ego extenders. He surely displaced this Christian hatred to the Jews, too. They were safe to hate and to destroy, especially in a population in which many members already displaced their hatred for Jesus to the Jew.

Once Hitler imbued Jews with the mythical power to rule the world, he believed and feared his own delusional lie. Growth of the lie in his psychotic imagination increased his fear, his hatred, and his envy. Yes, he suffered from a most degenerate form of envy. He wanted everything they had and more. He wanted to be them. He wanted to be what he came to believe as their supreme intelligence and Machiavellian, manipulative, omnipotent skills.

He wanted freedom from Christian restrictions so that he could fulfill sociopathic, narcissistic strivings without blockage by moral or ethical considerations. He believed that the Jews were free of these constrictions. He also believed that they functioned as a single, maximally efficient unit—a mystical cabal. He wanted that for his Aryan Germans. He wanted to be them and the more he invented about them, the more he became attracted to his own invention and the need to be them. But to be them he had to remove them—then he could make the transplant and replace them with himself. He could become *the chosen one*—not unlike scores of psychotic patients who believe the are Christ but who are neither sociopathic, have no special genius, are in the wrong time and place, and may not envy the Jews at all.

We may say that in Hitler we see the disease in metastatic, malignant macrocosm. Without large societal changes in terms of symbol sickness and particularly the Jew-hating dynamics, given a particular set of sociopolitical circumstances and charismatic, triple-factor leader—sociopathic, psychotic, mobmanipulator psychologist—another Holocaust is possible.

25 > WHAT ABOUT HITLER'S GERMAN PEOPLE?

The degree of inner deadening, low self-esteem, lack of spontaneity, lack of feelings and empathizing ability, lack of identifying values and inner structure, lack of human priorities, lack of moral and ethical consideration and judgment, hunger for dictatorial organization to combat feelings of inner disintegration, urge for conformity, lowered independency, paranoia, and self-hate must have comprised enormous symbol sickness in Germany during Hitler's time.

How else could a people identify with and follow the dictums of a dehumanized, grossly psychotic sociopath? The fact is that Hitler obviously embodied these pathological features to a psychotic degree. There was nothing subtle about his ranting. His psychosis was always visibly evident. Psychiatric expertise was not necessary to reveal it. Yet, the people followed because they, too, had the disorder. It couldn't be otherwise. Another population would have hospitalized him and certainly rejected him. Another population could not provide the necessary millions of people he employed in order to kill the Jews and at the very least to cooperate in the killing by turning a deaf ear.

All other aspects of symbol sickness must have been rampant, too. Otherwise ready volunteers who delighted in torturing and killing Jews could not be available in huge numbers. There must have been scores of men who were terrified of their own femininity. Polarized characteristics lending to deep and hated gender confusion must have been common indeed.

A penchant for law and order born of a terror of lack of inner controls fed morbid dependency and provided high suggestibility and a willingness to follow a deceptive and cunning liar.

I cannot believe all this was the result of a destructive World War I surrender or of the bitter economy that followed.

I do believe that a long history of militarism, nationalism, and distorted human values provide more of the answers. But I am neither an anthropologist nor a sociologist nor a political scientist and we require the wisdom of all disciplines to understand the evolution of a culture that so readily succumbed to the deepest and most monstrous psychosis and lack of conscience.

Obviously, the Germans were not alone in this regard. Ready converts existed in high numbers all over the world and especially in Europe, making metastatic spread of the disease easy. And, of course, there were others—many others, even great world leaders—who by their passivity also demonstrated considerable infection and affliction.

Obviously, symbol sickness—particularly this form of symbol sickness, embodying double feelings about Christ, profound envy, projection, paranoia, and self-hate—transcends national boundaries, educational levels, and even intelligence quotients.

Hitler readily found an entire population highly syntonic and therefore receptive to the vile exudates of his cancerous delusions. The simple fact is that paranoid leaders require paranoid cultures to spring from and from which to draw disciples.

Hitler believed his own hysterical rantings. These were not alien to him. Psychosis had robbed him of the ability to discern the irrationality of his thoughts and feelings. We all have irrational ideas but we know they are crazy. The ideas are ego-alien and a rational self much stronger than the aspect of self that is crazy views the craziness and rejects the craziness. In Hitler's Germany and elsewhere as with Hitler, there were many people whose rational selves were too weak, too small, or even nonexistent. As with Hitler, these people had become their irrational selves and in many cases murderous extensions of their hatred-ridden, megalomaniac leader. In these people compassion and empathy were dead!

In normal life, followers of leaders retain enough self so that separation from the leader continues as individual identity, regardless of fidelity to the leader, remains intact. But in psychosis, devotion often produces destruction of ego boundaries. We then see a folie en masse, in which an entire population acts as one monstrous organism as the leader takes over and virtually destroys the ability to equivocate individually on any moral or ethical level. Mob psychology is not unlike this phenomenon. This accounts for the mass suicide in Guyana at the direction of their leader, sociopathic and psychotic Jim Jones, and for the Eichmanns, and for the spread of virulent anti-Semitism.

A population brainwashed into authoritarian response—largely comprised of submerged, passive, morbid dependents, easily terrified by weakness induced by inner conflict, splits, polarized gender confusions, years of experience as automatant suggestible robots—such a population is ideal for germination and spread of the disease. Add a terrible economic situation, hurt national pride, poverty-induced grief, fear, ignorance, and long-standing Jew hating born of the dynamics discussed earlier and we have vast fuel waiting to be ignited by the charismatic lunatic leader.

26 > THE MOTHER RELIGION

A s I indicated earlier, Judaism is easily seen as the mother religion, for having given birth to Christianity and for exerting its enormous influence on Western law and culture generally.

Strange things happen in the unconscious since unconscious dynamisms do not have the benefit of conscious logic or the need for reality testing. But once confusions of unconscious forces take place, their influence on conscious beliefs and behavior can be enormous. This is especially true of very sick symbol sickness sufferers whose hold on reality is tenuous at best.

Therefore, let me speculate that there may be another dynamic involved in addition to anti-Semites' envious viewing of Judaism as original and their own beliefs as synthetic facsimiles.

I speak here of people who have strong unresolved oedipal conflicts, and considerable guilt, self-hate, gender confusion, and fear and hatred of women.

As a mother group, as the people who gave birth to mono-theism and Christianity and to much else and who continue to be productive and influential, Jews readily fit the role of mother.

As such, they then offer an easy target for displacement, and projection. Hatred for the mother is repressed to the un-conscious and projected to Jews on the conscious level. This projection would be fed by any disturbed relationship with parents or authority. Further hatred would be fueled by seeing Jews as the original parents of conscience and morality added to unresolved feelings toward parents for providing authority. To what extent, I wonder, may this particular dynamic have played a role in authoritarian Nazi Germany?

27 > DEADNESS, SADISM, AND JEWS

Being part of a distinct minority that is highly noticeable and often relatively helpless politically, the Jew becomes an excellent foil for the sadistic anti-Semite.

Some anti-Semitic symbol sickness sufferers and other bigots as well are particularly sadistic.

I view sadism as Karen Horney did. The point is to manipulate others, to hold power over them in order to feel more powerful oneself. But of even more importance, the object is to feel vicariously through others. Let me refer you back to my discussion of alienation in section 13, Chapter 2 on symbol sickness in Part I.

The sadist is a person whose feelings are blunted and even deadened. This kind of symbol sickness sufferer can almost have feelings himself by inflicting pain on others—a feeling that is almost palpable. This means that inflicting pain is a last-ditch attempt to have feelings vicariously oneself. Coupled with bullying tactics, the infliction of pain makes the sadistic bully feel momentarily alive and potent. This is compensation for feeling powerless, helpless, and dead.

Of course, if Jews live in a society where they are looked upon as venomous, less than human, and dangerous, too, sadistic acts will be rampant. Indeed, sadism may be condoned and rationalized as a worthy, macho kind of practice demonstrating courage and loyalty to the main group.

Obviously, there is great danger to Jews and other minorities where symbol sufferers abound who evidence much deadening of feeling. This occurs where there is much brutalization and much confusion as to what constitutes masculinity and strength. Gender polaization is usually quite evident in both the families and cultures in which sadism is commonplace. Child abuse emotionally even more than physically, and destruction to real self-esteem, is often part of the sadist's history. I wonder about the extent of sadomasochism in the German population during Hitler's time.

28 > EICHMANN, UNFAMILIARITY, AND NARCISSISM

We all seem to have difficulty with what is unfamiliar. Indeed, many of us have fear to the point of phobia of anything including people and cultures that are not familiar. This often prevents change and growth and produces deep resignation to the point of status quo stagnation and paralysis.

We cling to the familiar as if it is a lifeboat. Interest in the unfamiliar and optimism in this regard contribute to adaptability and the possibility of healthy change. I believe that the determining factor here is largely a question of self-esteem, a sense of strong personal identity and a lack of fear of dilution. Eventually, of course, with courage, we can take chances with the unfamiliar so that the unfamiliar becomes familiar. As it does, we become less apprehensive and even begin to generate feelings that are good—liking and even loving what was formerly unfamiliar. Not so with many anti-Semites!

There are some anti-Semites who have particular difficulty with the unfamiliar. As described earlier, poor self-identity is threatened by anything not completely understood or lending itself to mastery, thus rendering it impotent and of no dangerous consequence becomes all-important.

But there are some sick people particularly terrified of the unfamiliar. They are caught in a severe conflict. As they attempt to familiarize themselves, because their own attitudes are so shaky, they inadvertently begin to identify with and even begin to feel that they are *becoming* the unfamiliar object.

These people often employ an interesting narcissistic device in an attempt to feel less threatened by the unfamiliar—unconsciously, of course, and unwittingly. What they do is to incorporate the unfamiliar and hated object unto themselves so as to make it manageable—less abrasive, much as an oyster weaves a protective pearl around a foreign, irritating grain of sand.

The anti-Semite who does this is in fact incorporating and adding to his own identity that of the hated object—the Jew. Thus he takes unto himself increased self-hate. In an attempt to eject the hated object and to extricate himself from this torturous trap, he may (1) attempt to convince himself that the object—Jew—is even more unfamiliar and safely different from him; (2) that this alien is indeed a menace to his own well-being and safety; and (3) that eradication is necessary and constructive—whatever the rationalization (racial lies, etc.) he uses. These anti-Semites, I believe are people with particularly weak ego boundaries. They have no solid sense of self. They do not know where they end and the rest of the world begins. Their fluid boundaries make incorporations of others easy and a constant threat to their already very weak ego structures.

The arch war criminal, Adolf Eichmann, may well demonstrate this kind of variation of the disturbance, to which Hilter and others, as I pointed out earlier, were not alien either.

Eichmann was a severely alienated man. This means alienated from feelings, most of which were deadened. He was what I call a *natural good Nazi*. This means that he was a person with virtually no self, malignantly dependent and ready-made to be taken over and told what to do—the perfect automaton. He, of course, saw himself as the dutiful German soldier: perfect, perfectly without values, moral equivocation, conscience, or decision-making ability—the perfect lobotomized tool of greater will, the leader. In Eichmann's case (as with many morbidly dependent people), the leader and his policy became Eichmann's self.

Eichmann was given the job to familiarize himself with Jews so as to become an efficient exterminator. He did exactly what he was told, even learning Hebrew as well as Jewish culture, values, humor, etc. As a matter of fact, Eichmann spent a good deal of time in what was then Palestine to learn as much about Jews as possible, and he did a superb job.

I believe that Eichmann in familiarizing himself with Jews began to feel like a Jew and even perhaps began to like them. He probably began to feel that he was being invaded by the leader's enemy and becoming one of the hated. This brought Eichmann into severe conflict with his newfound self—the leader and the leader's policy and dictums. His terror could only be wiped out by wiping out his awakening feelings of humanity, by thoroughly destroying the Jews who stirred these feelings and who were the source of this unexpected conflict.

Is it possible that in Eichmann's case, familiarity led to liking and perhaps even love, reminiscent of feelings (getting in the way of authoritarian behavior); incorporation of the unfamiliar, becoming familiar; generation of intense conflict and fear of loss of (Nazi) identity and fear of fragmentation? Love now turned to hate and self-hate of a lifetime was joined with hatred of the now-familiar, formerly unfamiliar Jew. To annihilate his feelings and his conflict and to restore himself to his purely authoritarian automaton Nazi hero self and to his total submission to the leader and his dependency on the leader, he in fact used his familiarity with Jews to become one of their prime murderers.

It does not surprise me that many Jews and members of other minority groups become somewhat wary of people other than themselves who start liking them a lot. Unfortunately, some have experienced love turning suddenly to extreme hate, without knowing quite why.

29 > THE JEWISH ANTI-SEMITE

The Jewish Jew hater is always extremely self-destructive. I use the term *self* here quite literally. His destruction of self completes the severe emotional damage, especially to self-esteem, already inflicted during his formative years. He also has an enormous potential for destruction of his own people. Some of the cruelest and most fanatical destruction was the work of former Jews during the Spanish Inquisition.

Jews who hate Jews have invariably been severely emotionally damaged as children. They always suffer from very serious symbol sickness. A sense of self, a real value system, connection to humanity and the human condition generally are missing. Alienation from feelings, inner deadness, enormous self-hate, displacement, projection, and confusion are characteristic. There is frequently concomitant shallow or superficial living characterized by concrete, simplistic thinking as well as a high degree of conformity.

Many overtly, secretly, or unconsciously feel tainted by their Jewishness and blame limitations and difficulties on this accident of birth. Severe cases are, I believe, invariably psychotic.

Some Jewish Jew haters believe all they hear from non-Jewish anti-Semites and feel they must separate themselves from their pestilent birthright at any cost. Some are sociopathic, and enormous opportunism makes them dangerous to their confreres especially in times of mass anti-Semitic activity.

Jewish converts to other religions may not be anti-Semites at all. There have been very few voluntary conversions of Jews to other religions through the ages. But there have been some who through intense inner struggle came to embrace other philosophical and religious beliefs. These serious converts— as with serious converts from other groups—given enough health, are not inclined to be anti-Jewish or anti-anybody or anything else.

Zealots, especially Christian converts, can develop dangerous symbol sicknesses; symptoms may include the need to burn Jewishness out of their beings by burning Jews.

Some Jews have unfortunately internalized much of the hatred directed at Jews by anti-Semites. This, added to self-hate from other sources, may be unbearable. Hating Jews themselves is an attempt to obliterate their own Jewishness. Unfortunately, the attempt increases self-hate even as it fabricates a pseudo-self utterly lacking roots or meaning.

30 > NON-JEWISH, NON-CHRISTIAN COUNTRIES

What about societies where both Jews, Christ, and Old and New Testaments have had minimal roles and influences historically? What about places in which there are very few Jews?

They are not exempt! They, too, suffer from symbol sickness. Their populations also have their particular bigotries and groups singled out for persecutions under pressure.

The pressure here may come in the form of poisonous propaganda fed by members of already established Jew-hating societies. Thus, I have seen anti-Semitism in Chinese and Japanese Americans, who have only been in the United States one generation. There is also an increasing proportion of the disease in India and Japan, the former having a tiny Jewish population and the latter virtually none at all.

Without the input of the dynamics born of the Jewish-Christ connection, the tenacity, spread, and depth of the illness in Eastern society is questionable. But sociopathic opportunists, in quest of political power, know how to inject poison effectively.

Once the poison spreads and re-infection takes place continu-
ously by easy communication with Christian Western society,
the disease is very difficult to eradicate. In fact, it becomes easy
indeed to project difficulties to Jews by people who have little
or no contact with them. Their very distance makes it possible
to believe what one wants to believe and is told to believe, with
no interference by reality contact. Time and again I have met
people who were shocked when they found out that I was Jewish. Their shock really came from the fact that I was human
and that up to that point they had believed that Jews were otherwise. Obviously, they had met few or no Jews in their lives,
but had been thoroughly and adversely propagandized.

Thus, it is easy to see how an anti-Semitic book written by a
Japanese about a Jewish plot to control world economics is fast
becoming a Japanese best seller. If economic difficulties are en-
countered and sustained in Japan, the book may well become a
prime source of spurious expertise on Jews.

With a disease so popular in the West that it is not only
acceptable but often considered a normal condition, a special
influence is established. To hate Jews becomes a sign of being
updated, in the know, modern, smart, sophisticated, involved,
and even one of the good guys. To hate Jews means to be part
of the majority and not to be hated oneself. This is a form
of identification with the aggressor—in which strength is felt
through being "one of them." The ones in the majority and
the ones in charge are the ones to identify with. Unfortunately,
there were even a number of German Jews who early on felt
themselves more German than Jewish and believed they would
as Germans be safe. A few were even Nazi sympathizers—this
again I believe is an example of identification with the aggressor.

This appeal in some non-Jewish societies is attractive to people
who secretly see themselves as essentially weak and who are easily threatened. Societies given to macho, pride, sexist polarized
positions, authoritarianism, militarism, nationalism, and who

suffer loss of individuality are particularly vulnerable and are even more vulnerable where sexism and homophobia exist. Indeed, male pride-oriented societies may, after being sufficiently propagandized, see the Jew as impotent, feminized, submissive. This may guarantee a sustained anti-Semitism, even in societies that lack Judeo-Christian roots and have virtually no Jews of their own.

31 > EXCLUSIVITY AND PARANOIA

The Jews are not expansionists. They do not proselytize. They do not perceive God as issuing dictums to gather souls unto Him. Increasing their numbers through inculcation of nonmembers has not been a Jewish goal for thousands of years. They do not seek extension through marriage. On the contrary, they have tended to marry Jews whose values and customs they share.

Judaism is an ethical, value system, attempting to promote a righteous way of life. Righteousness largely consists of ethical considerations and values in terms of relating to people other than oneself.

The Talmud poses problems in the area of human relating and then attempts to analyze them, to extend them, and occasionally to resolve them. It is more interested in trends and directions than dictums. It is interested in extending human good for human beings and in change and growth along these benevolent lines. Compassionate and fair relating to one's fellows is doing the human work God intended. Understanding self is extremely important in this regard, not as a narcissistic preoccupation but to extend humility and insight. This is simply not the stuff of soul gathering! It is largely a here-and-now philosophy as part of a long continuum of heres and nows.

For Jews, the binding substance is comprised of common philosophical beliefs, values, and a rich subculture. The subculture has standards, language, humor, tastes, and I call it a *sub*culture because it transcends geography or political, national, economic boundaries or beliefs. In any case, there is no formal, discernible organization, centrality, chief person, or hierarchy. There is no missionary organ or ambition. There is no possibility of the existence of an organized cabal. Jews are Jews because they are born Jews, live as Jews, wherever they live and whenever they live. And they live also as Americans, Frenchmen, etc., too, and not because of any formal inculcation or homage paid to any centralized organization. Therefore, the Jew cannot conceive of inculcating anyone else. *I am because I am* is the raison d'etre and this is felt for oneself and is applied to everyone else as well.

In fact, I believe that the covenant between God and *the Jews* is not perceived as such at all. It is felt as a covenant between God and each individual Jew who feels entitled and even called upon to be with God in his own way. His entitlement springs from living life vis-à-vis other people—righteously, ethically.

This ethical living brings Jews a commonality shared by all and binds them together in a fabric that transcends place or politics. I believe it is this very *lack* of coercion and dictates that permits individual connection to God and makes powerful closeness to each other and to God possible. The Jew feels little coercion to rebel against his rabbi or anyone else. His rabbi has only been there to help him to resolve problems in ethical living and to find his own connection to God. In fact, there have always been two aspects of religious practices among Jews that interested me. First, though they congregate to pray together, they never seem to pray in unison. Each prays in his own way and his own rhythm. I remember always seeing some people cover their heads with a prayer shawl, constructing a private tent to pray separately under it as well as together in a synagogue with many others. Secondly, Dr. Marvin Weitz, who in addition to being a historian is also a rabbi, told me that requests of God are seldom encouraged, with only one exception. That request is for God's help to better understand oneself.

The victim of severe symbol sickness feels isolated, inadequate, rootless, and essentially without values or value. He would like importance. He would like notoriety, exclusivity. Even as he denigrates the Jews he envies what he sees as separateness, clannishness, and exclusivity. He believes that Jewish lack of interest in him, let alone winning him over, is a form of rejection. His reaction to rejection is enormous self-hate and projected self-hate. He rejects and despises the Jew, saving his own hurt pride and disguising his secret admiration and envy. He further embroiders the disguise, twisting envied Jewish characteristics into threatening ones. Thus, he sees Jewish commonality and cohesiveness as arrogance and unwillingness to meld and cooperate with the larger society. Even more, he sees Jewish cooperation and lack of missionary zeal or the desire to desire to assimilate as secretive, cabal-like machinations. These beliefs are illogically exacerbated and enlarged as Jews refuse to surrender their Jewishness and to disappear either through persecutory efforts on the part of the anti-Semites or through assimilation on their own part.

If the anti-Semite is sick enough, that is, sufficiently self-hating and paranoid, he will be convinced that the Jew is plotting against him and his. He then sees the Jew not only as a proud outsider, free of ordinary social restraints, but as part of a group organized specifically to carry out the plots against the insiders—rape, blood sacrifices, economic debacles, etc.

He sees Jewish intellectual interest and high educational motivation as part of the plot to get ahead and to rob him. High narcissism demands that he, the symbol sickness sufferer, is the center of Jewish motivation and function. Self-hate dictates that Jewish motivation is concerned with hating and hurting him. This provides a sense of importance and is consistent with feelings of fragility and an extremely weak and tenuous hold on who he is and what he has.

32 > ONSET, DEVELOPMENT, AND CONTAGION

The earlier the disturbance starts, as with most neurotic syndromes, the more difficult it usually is to eradicate. Unfortunately, as with most emotional difficulties, onset occurs early in life and then the illness becomes embroidered and metastasizes throughout the personality. This means that as the individual grows up, all that he perceives and his entire development is aberrated by the illness. Prejudice never remains encapsulated. It produces and aids distrust, paranoia, hierarchical thinking, hatred, self-hate, projected self-hate, etc., and is applied to groups and individuals alike. Even as it clouds vision, it absorbs energy, disturbs relationships, and deflects from constructive living on all levels.

As children, we are particularly susceptible to all environmental stimuli since we lack reality defenses born of experience in living. We combine high curiosity, high learning ability, and high suggestibility. Perhaps these are necessary in order to learn quickly and even more to incorporate unto ourselves values and lessons. This may enable us to cope with life as development and growth take place sufficiently to provide safe, independent autonomy. But high learning ability and suggestibility in the developing child can be counterproductive and severely damaging if what is suggested and learned is tainted by the distortions of great sickness.

Unfortunately, the dynamics of both symbol sickness and particularly the ones relating to Jew hating (Part II) are ubiquitous, and the child easily falls victim. When he does so at a very early age, the disease is so much a part of his developing structure that it's almost organic. Unfortunately, it takes hold and hangs on much as his tastes, values, and likes and dislikes do, all of his life.

The ability to be extricated from the illness will have much to do with how much constructive forces in his life remain intact and how great the possibility of contact with a constructive cultural environment exists. For example, during adolescence, time spent in Nazi Germany was disastrous. Time spent among a healthy, nonbigoted population is helpful. But what is brought to him via his own family is of paramount importance. This accounts for many German anti-Nazis whose own families transcended the disease in their nation.

There is no substitute for inner constructive forces that remain intact such as openness, high self-esteem, objectivity, love of people and the human condition, feeling a full range of emotions, lack of fear of the unfamiliar, independence, ability to cope with helplessness, high frustration and anxiety tolerance, etc. Unfortunately, where these assets exist in paucity or not at all, the sickness will prevail and will spread.

Spread takes place through one's own personality and to others as well. It takes place generationally as people become victims of victims, teaching each other the ways of the disease. In fact, there are many families of severe Jew haters in which there is no idea whatsoever that a sick process is going on. Jew hating is as acceptable and is seen as normal as breathing air.

Unfortunately, many of these victims are supported by a subculture that also feels the same way and often go to houses of worship in which Jew-hating sermons are considered normal and good.

Interestingly, many Jew haters, just as many envious people, have no idea at all that they are sick. But even more interestingly, they have no idea that they are either envious or that they are Jew haters. Many Jew haters repress their hatred of Jews, and when confronted with the reality of their anti-Semitism will actually deny it. One can readily see that the whole Jew-hating process, as with envy, may go on on a relatively unconscious level. Cultural acceptance of Jew hating helps idealize oneself as being a non-bigot even as one is a Jew hater, a peculiar split which permits self-idealization to take place even as the disease goes on on a relatively unconscious level. Thus we see top-level executives who somehow have a history of never hiring Jews and of belonging to clubs that do not accept Jews as members who deny anti-Semitic feelings.

Of course, large populations consist of individuals, after all. If symbols sickness is high on an individual level and the socioreligious factors are present, too, whole populations will indeed suffer from the disease.

Adult symbol sufferers are particularly susceptible to suggestion because, having deadened feelings and having poor and shaky values and high dependency, they can be readily swayed, especially if offers are made of scapegoats to absorb their considerable self-hate. If in addition they are opportunists who may gain by the demise of the Jews and even take over their property, as has happened in many countries over the ages, they will be particularly susceptible both in terms of their scape-goating needs and in order to satisfy their greed. Thus, there are many victims who become Jew haters in adult life who may come from families not particularly prone to the disease. However, in our society investigation of most anti-Semitic backgrounds I think will reveal at least some fragment of early background of Jew hating.

Thus, it can readily be sent that Jew hating is highly contagious, as is all bigotry. Once people become symbols, spread of prejudice and bigotry runs rampant. Extremely active application of insight and education is necessary to check the disease. Checkmate and eradication is extremely difficult and probably only possible if applied to the very young before roots of the disease take hold. Of course, this means application to parents even before they become parents and to all cultural institutions and influences, especially religious and educational groups.

PART III

33 > TREATMENT

It is not my intention to include details of treatment in this book, which as you have read is primarily a discussion of the dynamics of the illness.

But I feel that I would be remiss if I didn't mention a few thoughts that I have had in this connection.

I think that this pervasive illness is one of the most difficult to cure. Its tentacles are wrapped up in the very identifying structure of the individual. In effect, a desperate struggle must take place for a healthier reidentifciation to take place so that cure can take place.

Patients never present themselves for treatment of bigotry. But on occasion when they present themselves for treatment of other sympton complexes (severe depression), if treatment is thorough, it may also analyze and cleanse them of their bigotry. Unfortunately, unless a complete analysis takes place they may be relieved of their motivating complaint and leave treatment with their bigotry intact. When this happens they remain very sick people and are more likely to continue to have attacks of various emotional disorders. This rarely motivates them to analyze their bigotry.

Therefore, in this section my thoughts are mainly devoted to prophylaxis, approaches to children, and the long-range application to the illness as a worldwide problem.

34 > REALIZATION AND RECOGNITION

Most people do not realize that Jew hating is a disease process—a psychiatric disturbance. Even those people who abhor it seldom recognize it for what it is. They readily recognize the damage it inflicts on Jews—and I include Jewish symbol sickness victims themselves, that is, Jewish anti-Semites—but they do not connect Jew hating with sickness at all.

Moral and ethical equivocations about bigotry, historical documentation, socioeconomic studies, etc., usually do not address the problem of the illness. The black plague of the Middle Ages could not be eradicated or even attenuated until it was recognized that this was a disease process and it was connected to the causative agent—bacillus pastorelis.

Jew hating and all bigotry are psychodynamic illnesses and must be thought of as such if serious application to their eradication is to take place. This must happen as a two-pronged attack, addressed to the individual symbol sickness described in Part I and to the cultural dynamics that feed the disease, prevalent worldwide, described in Part II.

As with other illnesses, early realization that an individual is disturbed in this way is extremely important. This includes self-realization as well as early diagnosis in others as well as in children. Helping in any way at all, through communication and education and if necessary (if motivation is sufficient), psychotherapy can be crucial in preventing malignant development and spread.

Symbol sickness of more than moderate degree is prodromal but need not give rise to Jew hating. However, susceptibility runs high for the people who suffer from strong symbol sickness.

Seeing people in terms of group identification, generalizations about "them," and projections and displacements to "them," are always evidence of early disorder and often are evidence of advanced cases also. Without alertness to bigotry, without caring—these early diagnostic signs are easily overlooked, especially in societies where prejudice is taken for granted, accepted, and even condoned. Chronic "overlooking," even without active participation and contribution, is evidence of high susceptibility and even early stages of affliction.

Of course, there is a myriad of symptoms that constitute evidence of symbol sickness—undue depression, expressions of self-hate, chronic anxiety, phobic reactions, paranoia, chronic discontent, inability to tap one's own resources, inability to sustain relationships, etc. To the extent that these are recognized and appropriately treated, much of the neurotic germinating ground for bigotry is removed. This largely happens through removing the need for envy, illogical claims, abused reactions, displacement, and projection. It is valuable in this connection to remember that envy itself is a projective device that removes emotional and identifying centers of gravity from oneself and displaces the center of gravity to the person envied.

35 > MORE ABOUT MOTIVATION

As with all illnesses, especially psychiatric ones, motivation is crucial.

The anti-Semite is seldom, indeed is almost never, motivated to stop being anti-Semitic. Indeed, he feels utterly justified, righteous, and rational in his beliefs. He believes that the Jew is hatable and that his hatred is directly proportional to Jewish obnoxiousness and even criminal characteristics. He believes that every stereotype is true and sees every distortion and lie as a fact. He usually sees real facts proving that Jews are not at all as he believes them to be as lies, and even as further evidence of Jewish perfidy. He knows nothing and resists knowing anything regarding his own unconscious motivation or dynamics. He has no insight whatever that may shake his belief system, to which he clings tenaciously and which he nourishes.

Obviously, prophlaxis and cure must come from other sources.

People are motivated to prevent and help curtail disease in children and loved ones if they are convinced that they are in fact dealing with disease and that the latter is uttimately destructive.

The corrosive effects of self-hate, envy, distortion, and projection are obvious. Projection and displacement in all forms rob us of responsibility, healthy growth, and choice. Time and energy wasted in hatred precludes applications to self and mutual benefit. Symbol sickness is the stuff of chronic self-hate, the great robber of joy, and provides infliction of pain on others.

Prevention and eradication of these human enemies and the benefits derived are sufficiently motivating.

But what about goodness, the good feelings that come of being good, of being fair, and, yes, of loving the human condition in all of its diversity?

What about real moral and ethical considerations, those that militate against hatred? Don't we want this for our children and for ourselves?

There are, I believe, scores of us who still believe *in the incredible value of goodness*. Goodness precludes bigotry! Goodness means love thy neighbor as thyself and includes love thyself—have compassion for self and others. Blind chronic rage at others is the antithesis of goodness. The simple fact is that goodness is healthy!

When we are fair and good and accepting and gentle and loving, we are whole, energetic, vital, alive, in touch with our feelings and in touch with others. This is the antithesis of symbol sickness fragmentation, bitterness, cynicism, and paranoia. I believe that goodness, the greatest enemy of bigotry that selfishly attempts to rob others of the benefits of life, is the most therapeutic agent we have. In its presence we enjoy physical health, mental health, and the delights of small and large things. Our receptors and perceptions are better so that we can delight in food, air, water, vegetation, and people who are around us. In this state other people's self-realizations never feel as self-detractors or deprecators or as a personal assault on us, inflicting personal loss. We feel enriched by other people and their self-realizing accomplishments. Simply put, we feel related and as a family who makes diverse contributions.

So much for motivation.

36 > CULTURAL CHANGES

What societal changes would be helpful? Let me briefly list and describe a few. Without changes in this area, scapegoats will always be present. The disorder is rooted in the cultural matrix. True amelioration cannot take place without societal changes.

- The reduction of competitive striving and substitution of cooperative satisfaction.

  Competition is seen as a source of ego strength does not succeed and leads to emptiness. It is antithetical to love and the satisfactions derivative of cooperation. Hierarchical striving and positioning feed narcissistic pursuit. In competition, identification with the group is less influenced by constructive cooperation and occurs more through group antagonism toward other groups. This contributes to chauvinism, nationalism, prejudice, and paranoia— an ideal groundwork for bigotry.

Hierarchical striving against others must be replaced by satisfaction through self-realization of people other than oneself or one's group. I believe much of the source of competition comes from the area of sibling rivalry. I do not believe sibling rivalry is inherited or instinctual. I believe much sibling rivalry is engendered by parents themselves, often unwittingly. This occurs as they put one child up against the other in terms of winning acceptance from the parents through performance that is approved of. To the extent that an individual learns to cooperate with siblings rather than compete with them, they will be so much better off later on in cooperative and constructive relating on an adult level.

- Therefore, education about other groups, their contributions, the importance of richness derived from various cultures, the satisfactions derived from cooperation impacts on potential hatred. Familiarity is an antiparanoia device of some merit.

- Specifically, in this case, promoting understanding of Jews, who they really are and where they come from: the values they believe in, their commonality with non-Jews, their moral and ethical frames of reference, their Talmud and Torah, have major relevance.

- Christ was a Jew! He probably died a Jew. The New Testament is derivative of the Old Testament! Teaching these connections, I believe, can be highly constructive. It is especially important that children understand Christian roots and derivations on a fully conscious level and especially so the first time recognition of prejudice takes place.

- Humanization, compassion, empathy, and love comprise antihating machinery.

This is the stuff of real Christianity, Judaism, and all benevolent, people-welfare-oriented religions.

By humanization, I mean learning and having compassion for the human condition in all of its ramifications, including its tribulations.

Reality is helpful in prevention and treatment of all disturbances—especially this one. Learning about human limitations, confusions, and difficulties is helpful in understanding and accepting oneself and other people and increasing compassion. Reducing expectations dilutes self-hate and disappointment and helps to accept other people. Humility goes a long way to dilute humiliation of self and others. Reduction of glory seeking on every level—personal, ethnic, and national—is helpful.

Humanization (learning about the real human condition—especially its limitations) reduces claims on others, aggression, competition, and envy. Openness and trust are enhanced as paranoia is neutralized. Closeness, knowledge of others, increased familiarity, and friendship become possible as do empathy and sympathy. Commonality becomes evident even as differences are observed, respected, and are not regarded with contempt or suspicion. Camaraderie and communication are the enemies of bigotry.

I believe changes of this kind, indeed of any kind relative to this problem, must take place on a family level and as a governmental active policy. A few people of goodwill can do much but this is not enough in tackling this kind of metastatic problem. Governmental internvetion on a legal level is relevant, but programs designed to educate citizens can be an effective step by governments on all levels.

Teaching children compassion and respect for the human condition in all of its diversity and difficulties is a key prophylactic action. This must be done on an educational level and through family example.

Being responsive to the earliest manifestations of the disorder in children—tracing it down and removing sources and of course clarifying issues—is extremely important.

- Reduction of nationalism, chauvinism, group superiority, glory seeking, and aggression on all levels is vital!

- Promotion of the Judeo-Christian philosophy of brotherly love in all areas of life is enormously helpful.

- Depolarization of sexual characteristics; reduction and obliteration of fear of femininity and so-called feminine characteristics and interests and values; destruction of fear and hatred of women and passivity; obliteration of fear of homosexuality and homophobia; destruction of sexism on every level—all these are of vital importance, especially in preventing destructive acting out.

- Reduction of sociopathy and preoccupation with narcissistic gratification largely promoted through the media is extremely important.

Promotion of a value system that enhances self-esteem through contribution to society and to helping other people is enormously worthy but must start in early childhood.

- All bigotry is a related illness. Each form is related to underlying symbol sickness. It is always contagious. Susceptibility in competitive, sexually polarized, glory-seeking, narcissistic societies is high. Bigotry for one group can easily shift to another. Safety from the illness always involves eradication of bigotry in all forms against all groups.

37 > SOME DIALECTICS

Let me conclude with this brief final section by asking some questions, making a few parting comments, and adding some more questions. Perhaps some of my questions are somewhat Talmudic and generate more problems and still more questions. I hope they add some insightful direction as they in part summarize several pertinent aspects of the problem.

- Is it mandatory that scapegoats exist? Externaliza- tion, projection, and displacement are surely due to inability to take responsibility. Is this evidence of im- maturity and delusion as regards the human condi- tion and its imperfections and limits? Is this evidence of fear of self-hate generated by potential falls from glorifying self-idealization? Can projection stop in people who refuse to recognize and take responsibil- ity for their own inner conflicts and the anxiety these conflicts produce?

- Can bigotry be eradicated in a pride-oriented world in which hierarchical, competitive striving supersedes cooperative relating?

- The belief in a super being, God, dictates a position of anti-pride, anti-self-glorification, and humility. Indeed, the belief in God keeps many people from megalomaniac delusions of grandeur leading to the psychotic belief in their own godlike status. Isn't it strange then that this humility, this sanity-saving device leads to insane pride investments in particular ways of worshipping Him? Even as belief in Him produces humility, we kill because we are grandiose enough to believe that only our own believers are worthy of living.

- Who is more dangerous: the arrogant, vindictive, obvious, and active bigot or the passive, compliant, conforming, self-effacing non-person, person? Is the former really a more advanced stage of the latter?

- Does this disease as with other mental illness often reach a stage of compulsion at which point, free will and choice no longer exist? Are we then dealing with frank insanity? If so, even as self-protection and societal protection is necessary, is retribution and vengeance or treatment appropriate for bigots and sociopaths?

  If we despise the Jew hater as much as the Jew hater despises the Jew, do we negate Jew hating as a disease and preclude investigation and treatment?

  Is compassion for those of us who are sick enough to commit the most heinous crimes the real measure of humanity?

- Is the disease (as in Hitler's case) and other similar

sociopathic diseases so severe as to burn out even re-
siduals of humanity? If so, are we then dealing with
alien monsters? As monsters, should we not eradicate them? But in view of their human birth, do they
remain connected to us? Are they reminders to all of
us of our own vulnerability to similar diseases? Can
we destroy a disease by destroying the patient? Has
the disease so ravaged the patient that he is no longer
a patient?

• Have Jews given too much to the world? Does in
fact no good deed go unpublished? Are pride and
envy the principal imperatives in human behavior? Do they permit the practice of free choice
and free will guaranteed by the Constitution and
other documents?

• Are people aware that the most deranged people
look "normal" and know right from wrong? Very
sick people are compelled to do what they do despite moral equivocation even if they must and
can rationalize their actions. Knowing right from
wrong is a legal concern. In psychiatry, compulsion
is of much greater concern. The very sick, especially the acting-out sociopath, may still know right
from wrong. He may also think he knows why he
commits a wrong. But he rarely really knows why
he commits a wrong or the compelling nature of
his act. This lack of conscious real motivation defines him as crazy!

• It is interesting to note that Jews were the foremost
of ancient people to be concerned with symbols:
language and meaning. Such is the nature of oral
history and law—Torah and Talmud. Anti-Jews are
at one and the same time symbol sickness sufferers

and haters of people preoccupied with symbols, especially with gray areas of symbol use.

• Isn't understanding this disease and its sibling diseases a form of compassion? Can we understand it if we lack compassion?

• I believe this disease has no basis in reality. There is no justification for hating Jews on a rational basis. Jew hating is always irrational and is always based on self, subjective, neurotic, and psychotic logic born and supported mainly by unconscious dynamics.

  Histories of the Jews and persecutions of them, unfortunately, do not describe a history of the development of unconscious dynamics implicated in this ongoing plague. Studies of economic, social, political, and other trends through the ages cannot account for Jew hating because they only provide rationales for projection and envy and neglect.

• Is it possible that the symbol sickness victim hates Jews and blacks for a secret envy of what he perceives as their fully lived lives? He is removed from feelings (alienated). He is resigned and feels empty, stuck, and hopeless. He senses that there are many aspects of himself that will remain undeveloped, unrecognized, unlived. He is trapped and frozen by inner tyrannical dictates. He sees Jews and blacks as being outside convention and therefore free to live fully realized lives. He sees their relative open expression of feelings as unique aliveness and he envies and hates them and also blames them for his loss.

• While it is true that envy of the Jews goes back to pre-Babylonian days—envy of their history-keeping ability, of their cohesiveness, of their self-esteem expressed through their morality, etc.—didn't the full explosion of anti-Semitism occur with the Christian era?

- Degradation of a people is destructive in two ways: (a) it immediately hurts through prejudicial destructive treatment and (b) believing the myths of degradation, the persecutor can't stand living with the object of his scorn. Therefore, to protect his own standing he must remove, restrict, or annihilate the degraded symbol so that he may not identify with it.

- Repentance and atonement are largely Jewish inventions. Are these the beginnings of true compassion? Studying is considered most important—even more so than doing, since studying leads to doing (Rabbi Akiva). Peace above all was always considered the greatest blessing for Jews. Respect for life is enormous! Aren't these qualities embarrassing to macho-oriented people seeking glory through ruthless aggression and even death?

- Paul Johnson in his superb *History of the Jews* points out the following:

  1. Emperor Hadrian (Rome) about A.D. 130 saw circumcision as he did castration and forbade it on pain of death.

  2. The power of Jewish literature has been enormous since the most ancient times. The Jews wrote their history constantly and were always concerned with human affairs and the human condition. The Bible records, "But there is not merely good and evil in these historical moralities; there is every shade of conduct, and above all pathos, intense sadness, human love in all its complexity—emotions never before set down by

man. There is too a veneration for abstract institutions, a sense of national choices and constitu-
tional issues."

3. The earliest Jews did not believe "The Temple"
   was necessary nor any central place. Jews could
   practice their doctrine anywhere.

4. The term anti-Semite was not coined until 1879.

5. Pre-Christ Jews were hated for their being different, clannish, monotheistic, refusing to mix, and
   superior intellectually even to the Greeks and to
   Greek culture.

6. "Without a country, the world is home."

7. "From each according to his ability and to each
   according to his need" was a notion adopted by
   Jews before Christ (I might add that it and welfare
   obligations as well generally long predated Karl
   Marx, who is credited with the above. Welfare is
   always a threat to symbol sickness victims, who
   chronically feel depleted and who abhor being
   called upon for help or any kind of resource.).

8. The Moslems also had an early history of fluctua-
   tion between liberal acceptance and anti-Semitism.
   (They too had their paranoid megalomaniacs and
   need for scapegoats.)

9. Paul Johnson, regarding anti-Semitic outbursts,
   by Isabel and Ferdinand of Spain, writes: "But
   most of all, they were caught up in the sinister,
   impersonal logic of anti-Semitism itself." (I believe that the personal dynamics of symbol sickness as well as the special pathological dynamics
   of the disease are always present.) He also says

(p. 277): "The historical record shows, time and again, that it develops a power and movement on its own." (Yes, it is contagious, but, as with all other sickness, it must have a host in order to exist. Here the hosts must be ready to be infected by having their own necessary pathological components. Even in the worst times, healthy people do not succumb.) On page 498 he writes: "The German people knew about and acquiesced in the genocide. There were 900,000 of them in the SS alone, plus another 1,200,000 involved in the railways. The trains were one giveaway. Most Germans knew the significance of the huge, crowded trains rattling through the hours of darkness." "The Germans were beneficiaries of murder. Scores of thousands of men's and women's watches..." He goes on to describe the distribution of Jewish goods to Germans.

- The sick anti-Semite has sick pride invested in his beliefs, whatever he thinks they are, and usually feels they should be the only beliefs extant.

- In conclusion, what about the effects of a strong Israel and the eventual in-gathering of the Jews from the Diaspora?

I believe this will produce increased respect for Jews and less fear of them at the same time. This is so because most of the world can cope with militarism and aggression better than with peace and compassion. The latter is more threatening than the former and makes greater demands on self for impulse control, for control of sick pride, for insight, and for selfless understanding.

But if the underlying dynamics of symbol sickness and culture and religion persist, so will anti-Semitism. Envy, pseudo-Christianity, sexual polarization, gender confusion, etc., will continue to be a danger to Jews and to other groups of people as well.

What about the Jews themselves? With a strong Israel they will survive but they may become more like the largely nationalistic, militaristic world they lived in formerly, but this time with fewer of their own original values intact. I believe that the Diaspora made adaptability mandatory for survival. Adaptability may be diminished but it may not be as necessary either with a stronger Israel.